SELECTED PAPERS OF DONALD MELTZER

VOLUME 1

Books by Donald Meltzer

The Psychoanalytical Process *(1967)*

Sexual States of Mind *(1973)*

Explorations in Autism *(1975)*
*with John Bremner, Shirley Hoxter, Doreen Weddell, and
Isca Wittenberg*

The Kleinian Development *(1978)*
(3 vols: Freud, Klein, Bion)

Dream Life *(1984)*

Studies in Extended Metapsychology (*1986)*

The Apprehension of Beauty *(1988)*
with Meg Harris Williams

The Claustrum *(1992)*

SELECTED PAPERS OF DONALD MELTZER

VOLUME 1
Personality and Family Structure

edited by
Meg Harris Williams

THE HARRIS MELTZER TRUST

Selected Papers of Donald Meltzer in 3 volumes published in 2021 by
The Harris Meltzer Trust
60 New Caledonian Wharf
London SE16 7TW

Volume 1: *Personality and Family Structure*

British Library Cataloguing in Publication Data
A C.I.P. for this book is available from the British Library

ISBN 978 1 912567 84 3

Edited, designed and produced by The Bourne Studios
www.bournestudios.co.uk

Printed in Great Britain
www.harris-meltzer-trust.org.uk

CONTENTS

Permission to reprint the following papers is gratefully acknowledged:

Contemporary Psychoanalysis: 'Identification and socialisation in adolescence', 3: 96-103 (1967); 'The relation of splitting of attention to splitting of self and objects', 17(2): 232-238 (1981); 'Adhesive identification', 1(3): 289-310 (1975).

We would also like to thank the colleagues and editors who have contributed to collecting or previously publishing Meltzer's seminars and papers, as noted in individual chapters and including:

'Note on a transient inhibition of chewing' (1959), 'Positive and negative forms' (1970), and 'Models of dependence in a family' (1981) were first published in English in *Sincerity: Collected Papers of Donald Meltzer,* ed. A. Hahn (Karnac, 1994). 'The role of pregenital confusions in erotomania' and 'Repression, forgetting, and unfaithfulness' were first published in *Bulletin of the British Psychoanalytical Society* (1974); 'The aesthetic object' was first published in *Bulletin of the GERPEN*, Paris (1984);

'The evolution of object relations' was first published in *British Journal of Psychotherapy*, 14(1): 60-66 (1997).

D onald Meltzer (1923–2004) trained as a psychiatrist in the USA and moved to England in 1953 to have analysis with Melanie Klein. He became a training analyst for the British Society, which he left in later years owing to disagreements that began after Mrs Klein's death and that concerned both the ideas set out in his first books *The Psychoanalytical Process* (1967) and *Sexual States of Mind* (1973), and the Society's methods of training and selection of psychoanalytic candidates. His London teaching came to focus on the child psychotherapy training at the Tavistock Clinic, where he worked closely with Esther Bick and Martha Harris, whom he later married. He was innovative in the understanding and treatment of autistic children, as documented in *Explorations in Autism* (1975; with John Bremner, Shirley Hoxter, Doreen Weddell, and Isca Wittenberg). The history lectures gathered in *The Kleinian Development* (1978), together with the clinical applications discussed in *Studies in Extended Metapsychology* (1986), pioneered the understanding of the theoretical context and clinical relevance of the work of Wilfred Bion.

In 1976 he also wrote, in discussion with Martha Harris and at the request of the Paris-based Organisation for Economic Development, a significant small book on *The Educational Role of the Family* (originally titled *A Psychoanalytical Model of the Child-in-the-Family-in-the-Community*), an original application of Bion's model of learning from experience to understanding the child's wider environment. The thinking and non-thinking mentalities that conflict within the individual are also applicable to family situations with the ever-present danger of falling into basic assumption groupings.

Meltzer was passionate about clinical work and teaching, and said his primary talent was the ability to read dreams: 'dreams are my landscape'. Mainly with Martha Harris, he travelled and taught widely in many countries, valuing above all the richness and diversity of the clinical material. However he was also an original theoretician in his own right. His longstanding and well-informed interest in the philosophy of language and aesthetics illuminated for him the aesthetic nature of the psychoanalytic method and of the struggle for mental health, and these themes became dominant in *Dream Life* (1984) and *The Apprehension of Beauty* (1988; with Meg Harris Williams).

In *Dream Life* he links the art of dream-reading, including reading the analyst's countertransference dream, with the origins of language and of symbol-formation in general. He narrates the change in perspective from Freud's original theory of dreams as puzzles to be decoded, to seeing dreams as the 'generative theatre of meaning', evidence of the psyche's attempt to orient itself towards reality, internal and external. Mental growth takes place in the 'quiet chrysalis of dream-life'. In *The Apprehension of Beauty* and his final book *The Claustrum* (1992) he expounds his formulation of the 'aesthetic conflict' that lies at the heart of mental development, symbol-formation and object relations, beginning with the infant's response from birth to the enigma of the mother's beauty (the object's exterior) and unknown interior. This experience of contrary emotions sets in motion the desire for knowledge, as formulated by Bion in his L, H, K (Love, Hate and Knowledge), an imaginative conjecture now expanded by a deeper knowledge of infant observation. Meltzer came to see almost all psychopathology, including the intrusive penetrations of the claustrum, as essentially retreat from aesthetic conflict. In psychoanalysis, this struggle for the soul of the inner child focuses upon the analysis itself as the aesthetic object for both analyst and analysand, governing the 'conversation between internal objects' that enables them both to learn something new and interesting from the experience of the moment.

Meltzer was no more interested in a 'Meltzer School' than Bion was in a 'Bionian School'. In supervision he said his aim was not to instruct but to make himself and his own experience 'available' for students to select whatever was meaningful for them. His hopes for the survival of psychoanalysis rested on the capacity of the next generation to learn from their own experience, which includes, of course, the ability to be inspired by teachers, not only through personal communication but also through books which can themselves be containers of psychic reality. With each new edition comes the possibility of ideas being fertilised as they find a home in other minds and take on a future life.

Selected Papers

The present edition of Meltzer's papers is spread over three volumes, yet even so is only a selection. Some appear in his books in the same or similar form, or were given as talks in several places whilst he was working on the ideas. Here they are grouped loosely according to the main orientation of the paper, under the headings 'Personality and family structure'; 'Philosophy and history of psychoanalysis'; and 'The psychoanalytic process and the analyst'. Inevitably these categories are somewhat artificial, since they always overlap to a degree. However it seemed a possibly interesting way to immerse new readers in the experience of Meltzer's world-picture, or his picture of the inner world. Meltzer's style of delivery changes a lot over his career, becoming more poetic, simple and accessible, partly as a result of the huge experience acquired in giving off-the-cuff lectures which he always refused to write down beforehand. But his essential picture does not change, and even the influence of Bion from the mid-1970s takes the form of confirming and making more precise pre-existing ideas, as of course must always be the way with any subjective reading. There is thus something to be said for not following a chronological presentation but instead looking laterally for ideas and examples.

Volume 1

This first volume of Meltzer's Papers focuses on the subject matter of psychoanalysis: the nature of the mind as a container for psychic reality. The selection begins with some expositions of Melanie Klein's key concepts: the paranoid-schizoid and depressive positions, and the movement from an egocentric dependence on the object to a concerned, responsible dependence – the essence of the depressive position. Meltzer sees Klein's view of psychic reality as a 'spatial' one deriving from the infant's initial perception of the mother's body-as-the-world. This is not a matter of theory or dogma but is rather an integral part of her vision and manner of describing observed clinical phenomena. This vision becomes the foundation for his own later elaboration of different types of identification, in particular adhesive identification and the claustrum, which are both represented here, with an interesting variant in a short paper comparing paranoia to the structure of a Gothic cathedral.

The search for individual identity is described also in significant group contexts. A classification of the group and individual structure of the adolescent personality illustrates the developmental role of splitting processes and the dynamics of projective identification. This can be read alongside Meltzer's summary of the different types of learning that take place within family structures, most of which fluctuate in social reality. Pregenital confusions in these contexts may be compared and contrasted with those in erotomania in adults; while the 'adult part' of the personality, at any age, operates under the aegis of the combined object. This adult mode employs a work ethic in all fields, which for Meltzer makes the concept of sublimation redundant. And to the traditional Kleinian concept of splitting of self and objects is added the splitting of attention (in Bion's sense) which underlies the emphasis Meltzer lays upon the developmental quality of 'interest' in the psychoanalytic relationship.

Meg Harris Williams
Editor; author of *Donald Meltzer: A Contemporary Introduction*
(Routledge, 2021)

CHAPTER ONE

The paranoid-schizoid and depressive positions[1]

(1974)

The subject I have been asked to talk about today is for many the most central of the psychoanalytic developments linked with the name of Melanie Klein. As with all psychoanalytic concepts it seems to me that, to understand their significance, we have to put them in the context of their history. And studying the history of Mrs Klein's ideas is different from studying that of Freud, owing to the fact that Freud is both a clinician and a theoretician, whilst Mrs Klein is almost exclusively a clinician who describes far more than she theorises.

The evolution of Freud's thought is like a country that underwent two revolutions: the first being the fall of the theory of hysteria, and the second being the overthrow of the theory of the libido in the 1920s and its substitution by the structural theory. The work of Melanie Klein on the other hand has grown in a way more analogous to the peaceful transformation that is characteristic of English political institutions. It seems to me that Melanie Klein, not having a particularly theoretical

---

[1] A talk given in Novara in 1974. First published in English in *Adolescence: Talks and Papers by Donald Meltzer and Martha Harris* (Harris Meltzer Trust, 2011).

mentality, did not particularly take account of the changes that were taking place in her use of terminology, and the theoretical implications that she was putting forward.

First I shall describe a way of viewing the conceptual changes that lay behind the formulation of the paranoid-schizoid and depressive positions, and then I shall link these to the problem of how to deal with adolescence as a period marked by specific points of change: first the transition from latency to puberty, then the transition from puberty to adolescence, and finally the transition from adolescence to adulthood. Let me underline some theoretical elements that help us to understand these transitions, and then describe the clinical implications of a move from the paranoid-schizoid to the depressive position, after which we can discuss technical problems occurring in your clinical work.

Melanie Klein entered psychoanalytic practice in 1919–1920 just at the time when Freud was starting to change the libido theory into what would later become the structural theory of psychoanalysis. It is important to try to see how the work of these two people links up and also how it is different. The fundamental difference is that Freud's approach was essentially a way of understanding psychopathology, and reconstructed infancy in retrospect; whilst Melanie Klein's approach originated in her interest in the development of babies, and then investigated the connection between this and the psychopathology of adult life. The reconstruction of infancy made by Freud lacks something which actual babies in their relation to the world could demonstrate in flesh and blood. The work of Melanie Klein on the other hand makes too little distinction between evolutionary conflicts and pathological processes.

When Mrs Klein started work in the 1920s, as we know, she began by observing the development of babies and then gradually adapted the psychoanalytic method to the treatment of children. At that time, in terms of theory, she was working primarily with Freud's ideas as modified by Abraham. These included the progression of the erogenous zones, and the pregenital organisation and then genital organisation of the libido; and at this time pregenital also meant pre-oedipal. At this time Freud or more particularly Abraham retained the idea that the oedipus complex only started in the genital phase of the evolution of the libido. Thus the first contribution of Melanie Klein to analysis falls into two categories: the first (for many the most important) was her discovery that babies are much preoccupied with internal spaces of the body, particularly of the mother and of themselves. Freud never conceptualised this. The second (as a result of babies' interest in these spaces) was the new concreteness given to the concepts of introjection and projection that Freud had already described. Melanie Klein was thus able to delineate the phenomena that she called the 'early Oedipus complex'. This was different from Freud's view not only in its description of a stage earlier than the development of partial objects, but also because it gave a greater psychic reality to internal objects than either Freud or Abraham had been able to fully conceptualise.

In the course of this Mrs Klein noted the sadism of babies, which gave her the impression that these phenomena began in the earliest stages of infancy, and she started to use the term 'position' for the first time. At first she used it in a variety of ways. She mentions a depressive position, an obsessive position, a maniacal position, a paranoid position. By the last she seems to refer to the anxieties connected with sadism and specifically organisation of defences against these anxieties. At this stage in her thinking the term 'position' is used almost exclusively in a descriptive sense, and is applied to almost any type of anxiety and defence related to the two periods of intense sadism of early infancy: oral-sadistic and anal-sadistic. In 1930, writing on manic-depressive states, Klein started to use the term in a more specific way, and in the two papers on manic and depressive states (Klein 1935, 1940), she used the term 'position' in a way that linked with Freud's theory of fixation points, to describe certain states as points of fixation peculiar to schizophrenia and manic depression.

In this period (the 1930s) she was talking of three positions: paranoid, depressive, and manic; and I think that at this time she maintained explicitly that in these respects the mental state of babies is fundamentally the same as that of adults. This one can say is the psychopathological phase of the use of the term 'position'. Klein talked of babies who 'overcome' the position in a way analogous to the way Freud talks of 'working through'. She tended to talk as though babies suffer from illness equivalent to schizophrenia, mania and depression, and was criticised for having concluded that babies suffer from mental illness. By the time she wrote 'Notes on some schizoid mechanisms' in 1946, her use of the term 'position' was becoming restricted to 'paranoid position' and 'depressive position'. Gradually she started to join paranoid with schizoid, differentiating it thereby from Fairbairn's concepts. Refining her picture of the emotional qualities of these positions, she became less exclusively preoccupied with sadism and its consequences and came instead to refer to love for the primary object in order to distinguish the states of mind which are preoccupied with the good health and survival of the object, not only of the baby.

So she began to describe the central nucleus of the depressive position in terms of 'pining' – a feeling of loneliness, mourning, regret, and awareness of separation. This seems to me to be a very important turning point in her thinking: added to the idea of love in the depressive position as centring on the object rather than the self. Such a change brought to psychoanalysis a vision of love which has no place in Freud's theories, which were from the beginning based on the idea of gratification of the libido.

Later Klein hypothesised that love might triumph over the narcissistic impoverished libido, consequently benefiting the ego. So while the first use of 'position' was an evolutionary one linked to the idea of defence, and the second use was linked essentially to psychopathology and the concept of fixation, the use of the term in the 1940's and thereafter placed such concepts in the field that one might call 'economic'.

But this also changes completely the meaning of the economic concept in metapsychology. For Freud, an economic concept was about quantitative aspects of the distribution of the libido and its vicissitudes. Its roots lay in his neurophysiological model of the mind and in the idea of quantities of excitement. One of the revolutionary elements one finds in Freud is his determination to establish a mental science free from moralistic prejudgements; and in his efforts to avoid assigning a particular weltanschauung to psychoanalysis one might say he proceeded in a manner that was non-moralistic to the point of being cynical. This is not to say that in his clinical work he was cynical or amoral; in studying his clinical cases, in particular the Rat Man, it is evident that his work is completely free from cynicism. Notwithstanding this, right to the end of his life – even after the new theory of the life and death instincts – he tended to try to integrate psychoanalytic thinking with biology in a way that might eliminate any philosophical standpoint or almost any idea of values.

It seems to me that the initial work of Melanie Klein faithfully follows this pattern: in her description of sadism in babies there is not the slightest trace of moral preoccupation. The baby's pain is seen as deriving exclusively from the feeling of persecution; the conflict between love and hate is related almost exclusively to the wellbeing and happiness of the baby; and the child that is exercising his sadistic impulses (in reality or in imagination) suffers from persecutory anxieties. In Klein's original idea of the depressive position, he seeks to escape these feelings of persecution by making 'restitution' as she called it. This meant essentially to give back what he had stolen and put together what he had broken. Gradually 'restitution' turned into 'reparation'; and reparation meant repairing the damage in order to avoid persecutory anxiety.

In the second phase of her use of the term 'position' – the psychopathology phase – Klein uses 'reparation' in a way which makes it indistinguishable from that which she afterwards called 'manic reparation'. She specified that this manic reparation is motivated essentially by omnipotence.

In the third phase of the use of the 'positions', beginning with writings on mourning and continuing with those on schizoid mechanisms, there is a slow and gradual change. By the time of *Envy and Gratitude* (1957) and 'On Loneliness' (1963) the entire approach has changed. The paranoid-schizoid and depressive positions start to lose their evolutionary specificity. She no longer describes them as something which occurs at the third month of life and resolves around the time of weaning, but starts to consider them as a type of mental conflict which has its origin around the third month but continues for the entire life of the individual.

The depressive position therefore is no longer described as something which is to be overcome, but something which is entered into. The movement between paranoid-schizoid and depressive positions begins to be seen as a continuous oscillation in the sense later delineated sharply by Dr Bion as Ps↔D. The concept of love is modified to mean that concern for the wellbeing of the object, predominates over concern for the comfort of the self.

I have said this is an economic concept, but a qualitative one. This does not in my view replace the quantitative economic concepts described by Freud, but is in addition to them. If one takes the economic concepts and tries to put them in meaningful order, one would put it like this: the most primitive economic concept is the repetition compulsion; this is the main economic principle of the Id, that knows nothing other than the repetition of previous experience and past activity, directly connected with physiological processes. The pleasure principle modified by the reality principle is the main economic principle used by the ego in its attempt to govern relations with the Id, as distinct from the external world. This is, one could say, purely narcissistic, in the sense of Freud's 'primary narcissism'.

But the paranoid-schizoid and the depressive position are the main economic principles of relations with the object. The paranoid-schizoid position is a value system in which the health, security and pleasure of the self dominate, whilst the depressive position is a value system in which the health, security and happiness of the object prevail. So in the later work of Mrs Klein the paranoid-schizoid and depressive positions have no special tie to evolutionary phases of development, nor any specific tie to pathological configurations; they are of general economic reference to all developmental phases and all psychopathological configurations. The concept of reparation also takes on a new significance, not as something that the baby is able to do actively, but as something which he permits to happen by restraining his destructive impulses. Reparation comes to be the precise opposite of destructive impulses and is connected very directly with the concept of integration.

In her paper of 1946 on schizoid mechanisms, Melanie Klein describes the two principal techniques by means of which disintegration comes about – through splitting processes, and through projective identification. These are truly named 'schizoid' mechanisms, and are the means by which the paranoid-schizoid position comes to be built. Reparation may be considered the principal depressive mechanism and in many ways the neutralisation of schizoid mechanisms. Thus that which has been split in schiz-oid mechanisms is reunited, and that which has been projected through projective identification is taken back inside.

These are the active components of the depressive position and are accompanied by depressive pains of various types: they form a spectrum that extends from feelings of regret, remorse, guilt at one end, to feelings of loneliness, depression, and pain at separation, at the other. She came to hypothesise that the self, when it becomes capable of playing its part in reparation, puts back together that which has been split inside itself, and recovers parts that had been projected outside, suffering feelings of depres-sion because of the damage it had done; whilst at the same time, owing to the feeling of loneliness, it now experiences the objects as separate from the self and this triggers a reciprocal reparation. This situation in which the self reunites split parts and suffers depressive pain, while the parental figures are separate from the self and united in a reparative sexual rapport, is opposed to the paranoid-schizoid conception of the primal scene in which the self intrudes into the parents' sexual union and stimulates a state of excitement, envy and jealousy in which schizoid mechanisms are operative.

With this conception of the paranoid-schizoid and depressive positions as the main economic principles that regulate and one might say direct the developmental processes, one can from the clinical point of view examine almost any developmental crisis in terms of transitions and oscillations between paranoid-schizoid and depressive positions. This is the meaning of Bion's little dia-gram Ps↔D with the double arrows. And it is from this point of view that we wish to examine the processes of transition that they illuminate between puberty, adolescence and adult life.

Before going on I will highlight some points of delicate equi-librium between the paranoid-schizoid and the depressive posi-tions. One concerns the use of the term 'guilt'. Guilt as it appears in depressive anxiety is rather more serious than regret or remorse, and probably involves the fear of having caused irreparable dam-age to the object. Guilt brought to light clinically in the analytic situation tends to be seen as persecutory guilt, and links with Freud's concept of the cruelty of the superego that results from quantities of aggressive impulse generated by the self. Klein has described this in more detail from the structural point of view. The cruel superego that produces persecutory guilt may derive from three sources: the first being splitting and idealisation of the object into idealised object and persecutory object.

The second source of persecutory guilt is projective identification of the bad parts of the self into the object, maybe then recombining the bad part of the object with the bad part of the self. The third source derives from the damaged object: the object seen as damaged in an irreparable way by the sado-masturbatory attack. Gradually the work of Melanie Klein was developing, and reached its most evolved form in the *Narrative of a Child Analysis* (1961) and in *Envy and Gratitude* (1957). This last category of persecutory guilt, felt as having caused irreparable damage of the object, seems in her clinical descriptions to centre itself ever more closely on the killing of the babies inside the mother.

The other point of delicate balance in the relation between the paranoid-schizoid and the depressive positions concerns the concept of reparation. Of the four types of reparation, two seem to lend themselves to the description 'false'. One type is described very clearly by Melanie Klein as 'manic reparation' in which omnipotence is used to try to reverse the damage done to the objects. The second is another type of false reparation, connected with what Mrs Klein initially called 'restitution'; it is insincere, like stealing a bottle of wine, drinking it and handing back the empty bottle.

CHAPTER TWO

From pain-and-fear to love-and-pain

(1980)

In the three previous chapters[1] I have described first, the psychoanalytic method in its excellence and limitations. Next, I traced Freud's early discoveries about infantile sexuality and his theories about the development of children particularly in so far as it forms the background for pathological symptoms in adult life. In Chapter 3, I outlined the sudden and unexpected development, largely due to the work of Freud and Abraham in the post-World War I years. This transformed psychoanalysis from a method for investigating and treating nervous illness into a special branch of psychology, *metapsychology*. A new, multi-dimensional and coherent conception of personality development took shape in terms of developmental phases and organisational series.

But I ended with a note of semi-apology for the living child who could not be found among the ponderous theories. I did however promise to remedy this defect by describing the developments between 1926 and 1946 which grew out of the direct analytic work with children, and especially the work of Melanie Klein with very young children.

1 Published in *Sexual States of Mind*, 1973.

Much of the impetus for this direct approach to the child had come from an unusual bit of work by Freud himself, reported in 1909 (*SE,* X) and known to analysts as the case of 'Little Hans'. This little boy of five, suffering from a phobia of horses but generally a healthy, intelligent and normal child, was not treated by Freud but by the child's father, who was acquainted with the findings of psychoanalysis, under Freud's close supervision. The clinical result was highly satisfactory, but left Freud very doubtful that such a treatment could be accomplished by many parents or by an analyst directly. It was only the development of modified technique by the three women I have mentioned, the so-called 'play technique', that made the direct treatment of children by the rigorous application of the psychoanalytic method possible. While Anna Freud at first advocated only a partial application of the method as compared with the more meticulous use of the transference by Melanie Klein, over the past 30 years these technical differences have largely disappeared. The advances of theory which partly resulted from this work, along with discoveries from adults, now make it possible to bring the psychoanalytical method to bear with some degree of success on all personality disorders of children from age two onward.

The case of little Hans did much to reassure Freud and his circle that their reconstruction of the oedipal period and the so-called 'infantile neurosis' which had been hypothecated as a precursor of the later adult neurosis – that this infantile edition of the disturbance did in fact exist. The case helped to infuse the theories of bisexuality and ambivalence with vitality, as a real little boy, struggling with his love and hatred of mother and father and with his own male and female genital desires, came to life in Freud's beautiful paper, probably the most delightful in the entire psychoanalytical literature. To Freud's power as a scientist was mated a rich literary genius which makes his works, either in the original German or in the faultless translations of James and Alix Strachey of the *Standard Edition,* truly part of the world's great literature.

Melanie Klein possessed no such literary gifts. The blunt, staccato and excessively condensed style of presentation of her early findings in *The Psychoanalysis of Children* (1932) did nothing to assuage the opposition to her ideas. While Little Hans had danced across Freud's page like a troubled little prince, poor Rita, Trude, Erna, Peter and others of the eighteen cases cited by Melanie Klein emerge as grossly abnormal, monstrous in their preoccupations and frightening in their violence. The explanation is, of course, not literary alone, for indeed these children were seriously ill, already enmeshed in disturbances which could only have led to severe neurosis or psychosis in adult life. In addition, the very nature of their illness involved the more primitive, more violently ambivalent, more dehumanised part-object levels of their mental life concerned with their pregenital organisations. Consider an excerpt, for instance:

> Trude, aged three and three-quarters, used repeatedly to pretend in her analysis that it was night-time and that we were both asleep. She then used to come softly over to me from the opposite corner of the room (which was supposed to be her own bedroom) and threaten me in various ways, such as that she was going to stab me in the throat, throw me out of the window, burn me up, take me to the police, etc. She would want to tie up my hands and feet, or she would lift up the rug on the sofa and say she was doing 'po-kaki kuki'. This, it turned out, meant that she wanted to look inside her mother's bottom for the 'kakis' [*faeces*], which signified children to her. On another occasion she wanted to hit me in the stomach, and declared that she was taking out my 'A-as' [*stool*] and was making me poor. She then seized the cushions, which had repeatedly figured as children, and crouched down with them behind the sofa. There she exhibited every sign of fear, covered herself up, sucked her fingers and wetted herself. She used to repeat this whole process whenever she made an attack on me. It corresponded in every detail with the way she had behaved in bed when, at a time when she was not yet two, she had been overtaken by very severe night terrors. At that time, too, she had run into her parents' bedroom again and again at night without being able to say what it was she wanted. Analysis showed that her wetting and dirtying herself were attacks upon her parents copulating with each other, and in this way removed the symptom. Trude had wanted to rob her pregnant mother of her children, to kill her and to take her place in coitus with her father. (Melanie Klein, *The Psychoanalysis of Children*, 1932, p. 25)

This is an uncompromising presentation which runs counter to whatever may remain within us of the tendency to idealise children or to see childhood as innocent, happy. How different from Little Hans, whose manly desires growing out of admiration for his father, to be big, to have a big fine penis and to marry his beautiful mother tend to bring approving smiles and nods of encouragement from us.

Still, here in a case like Trude, was rich confirmation of Freud's and Abraham's theories about the infantile roots of obsessional neurosis, the anal-retentive stage, the part-object nature of the relationships in this highly ambivalent pregenital organisation. And as such, naturally these findings with young children were welcomed into the literature of psychoanalysis. But it can easily be seen that such findings contain more than mere confirmation of theories derived from adult work. They reveal the pain in the ill child and demand our attention. This imperative could not really stand side by side with the Dickensian idealisation of childhood which viewed suffering as coming only from the outside, to orphaned, ill, handicapped or neglected children. It demanded recognition that children do not emerge from a cocoon of bliss into the ordeal of school age, but are born into a bedlam of infantile anxieties, in the midst of which their only oasis is the physical presence of a beloved or at least trusted adult. Every area of their daily life – eating, sleeping, playing, urinating, defaecating, learning, being bathed, dressed, or treated for physical ills – each was seen to be molested with anxieties of a type seen with adults only in the most severe mental disorders, the 'psychotic anxieties' of persecution.

Freud had taken the view, derived from his work with adults, that the institution of conscience, which he called the 'super-ego', developed as the 'heir to the Oedipus complex': that is, that the resolution of this infantile conflict of love and hate took the form of the establishment of the parents, and particularly the parent of the same sex, as an internal figure which functioned as a conscience. His studies of disorders more serious than hysteria, such as obsessional neurosis, manic-depressive states and schizophrenia, had shown him that they involved very severe disturbances of this structure, the super-ego, especially in the form of its being excessively harsh, even savagely murderous. But since these illnesses did not seem to appear until later childhood in the case of obsessions or adolescence in the case of schizophrenia, he concluded that the alterations of the super-ego occurred at these later times. He therefore saw no reason to modify his views about the time of origin of conscience, even though he recognised that the so-called 'fixation point' of these illnesses lay in the pregenital phases of development, i.e., generally prior to age three.

Consequently, the second significant modification of the picture of early childhood which came from Melanie Klein's work with young children was the recognition that the internal world of the child was already, or perhaps *especially*, at this early age highly complex, peopled in the child's conscious and unconscious phantasies by figures good and bad with whom it was in a constant state of conflict or alliance, ever shifting. Whether the many figures, linked in such important ways to the father, the mother and to various parts of their bodies, should be called collectively the 'early super-ego' or merely 'super-ego precursors' is not one of great importance today, but fierce battles raged over it in the years following Freud's death. The really important modification of our view of children was the growth of the rich concept of 'psychic reality', which is by no means a mere euphemism to imply that children set great store by phantasy. It is a rigorous scientific concept which recognises that the growth of a child's mind takes place through a continually oscillating process, in which his activities with figures in the outside world modify the qualities of internal figures, in conscious and unconscious phantasy. Play, dreams, phantasy, masturbation and other types of auto-erotism, in turn affect these internal figures and thus alter the child's view of the outside world in respect of values and meaning.

Let us go back for a moment to Melanie Klein's description of Trude's play representation of her night terrors. These had taken shape at a time, around age two, when her mother was pregnant. Trude's masturbation phantasies, in which she robbed her internal mother of faeces, babies and riches changed her mother into a frightening persecutor. This internal situation caused her to have night terrors which were inconsolable because her trust in her external mother was interfered with by a view confused with her internal situation. This made her wet and soil herself, which in fact caused some difficulty with her mother in the outside world;

this in turn increased Trude's envy and resentment, her tendency to masturbate, and so on.

A certain amount of disagreement still exists in psychoanalytic circles concerning the date of onset of these internal relations, the formation of this world of 'psychic reality', for again Melanie Klein in her uncompromising fashion insisted that the evidence indicated that these processes commenced with the very beginning of postnatal life. The exact dating is of little consequence for our purposes here. What matters is the recognition of the immense importance to the child's mental *and physical* development of this interior world of the mind, peopled with a host of objects, good and bad, which only very slowly and incompletely are integrated to form the parental figures of Freud's 'super-ego'.

I wish to stress 'good and bad' because this brings us to the third great modification of our image of children's mental life, derived from the work of Melanie Klein, in a way the most important from our point of view here, of bringing the child to life amongst the theories. In the eleven-year period bridging World War II, 1935 to 1946, in four monumental papers she formulated what are known as the concepts of the *paranoid-schizoid* and *depressive positions* in object relations, which, to my mind, have brought psychoanalysis into the most intimate relation to the pulse of life, the drama of love and hatred, good and evil, creation and destruction, growth and decay, beauty and ugliness, sanity and madness in individuals and in societies. The presentation of these concepts forms the finale, the coda of these historical chapters and requires a certain poetic flight to capture their beauty.

From her work with young children, and later with very ill adults, Melanie Klein concluded that the war between love and hate and between good and evil commences at birth or shortly thereafter that the pain and fear, and the rage which accompanies them, threaten the infant's desire to live to an extent which is a serious threat to its ability, in fact, to survive. If it is to survive in a reasonably healthy way, it must deal with this terrible state by a mechanism called splitting, whereby it divides itself and its objects most severely into idealised 'good' and persecuting 'bad' segments. The idealised 'good' parts of the self attempt to ally themselves with idealised 'good' objects, in the first instance with the feeding breast of the mother, or its representative. These are internal processes. A fundamental alliance, the mother–child idealised, forms the proto-type for the development of love, trust, gratitude and hope.

But this alliance, the idealised relationship, is threatened from all sides, both internally and externally. Every pain, disappointment or shock attacks the trust in the goodness and strength of the object. Every separation brings loneliness, jealousy which attacks gratitude. Envy of the goodness, beauty, strength or competence of the object works against the love. Any sign of wear, weakness or aging undermines the hope.

What I have described so far is the paranoid-schizoid position, in which all safety against persecution, pain and death is felt to derive from the strength and services of these idealised objects, at first the mother's breast, then a more coherent concept of the mother, later the father as well, and so on. But the accent is on being protected from pain and danger. In this organisation of the personality the good objects are valued, even loved or worshipped, but for their services – in a word, selfishly. At its best this orientation achieves an enlightened self-interest, akin to the benevolent despot's attitude to his subjects. It cannot experience *concern*.

Where this primary splitting and idealisation of infant self and objects has satisfactorily taken place, where the parental services are reasonably adequate, where neither jealousy, envy nor intolerance to mental and physical pain are excessive, a miraculous and beautiful thing tends to take place, known in flat scientific jargon as the 'phenomenology of the threshold of the depressive position'. In the language of life, tender concern for the welfare of the beloved object tends to supersede selfish concern for the comfort and safety of the self. The capacity for sacrifice emerges – babies wait for their feeds instead of screaming, leave off sucking when more is still available in breast or bottle, try to control their sphincters to spare the mother, bear separation despite worry. Out of obedience, goodness emerges; out of competitiveness, the capacity to work; out of toleration of deprivation, pride in development.

The beauty of these concepts helps us to see how children struggle, to comprehend their failures and their need to try again and again. At every juncture of a child's life he is presented with the dual problem of renouncing old services and developing new skills. At every juncture he must decide again whether to go forward or not, and, if forward, for what reason: enlightened self interest, fear, competitiveness – or concern for his good objects. Note that these concepts do not supersede the developmental stages and phases of organisation discovered by Freud and Abraham. Rather they explore the method of transition from phase to phase, and why at times development fails, how one failure increases the likelihood of the next, etc. These concepts are therefore primarily economic concepts, although we no longer think of 'psychic energy' as an analogue of physical energy. They are 'economic' not in a narrowly quantitative sense but more in the sense that a government may be said to have an *economic policy*. The economics of the self in relation to internal objects is governed in this way (via the principles of repetition compulsion, pleasure-pain-reality, paranoid-schizoid positions, etc.).

The child's struggle to preserve his relations to his love objects, both internal and external, involves him in problems that bring into focus the attributes of courage, for time and time again the child will fail to preserve good faith at the level of the depressive position and will be faced with the pains of guilt, remorse, unworthiness, shame. Time and again his love will bring in its wake increments of powerful worry, loneliness, and jealousy during separation. When we understand how dearly little children must pay for their love relations in the face of their limited self-control, it helps us to be patient, to support them with resolution, to protect them from undue hardships or temptations. These concepts show us as adults the need to exemplify in our behaviour, if we can, qualities like courage, integrity and capacity for sacrifice which can be assimilated to strengthen the goodness of the child's internal objects upon whom they must, during separation and eventually, totally, depend for support.

Here then, these three developments – the revelation of early psychotic anxieties, the establishment of the overriding importance for development of 'psychic reality' and the delineation of the economic concepts of paranoid-schizoid and depressive positions – are the discoveries of Melanie Klein, from 1921 to 1946, which have so greatly altered our understanding of the minds of children, and thereby changed so radically our judgment of the meaning of their behaviour.

CHAPTER THREE

The consequences of Mrs Klein's spatial revolution[1]

(1979)

Tonight I want to talk about spaces as implied and developed in Mrs Klein's work, and people who've taken off from her work. And then I want to talk about the way in which this seems to me to have developed in various directions. One direction is in the investigations of spacelessness and dimensionality that I and some of my colleagues wrote up in the *Autism* book, which you may have had a chance to see. Another is the direction taken by Mrs Esther Bick's work about skin containment and adhesive identification. And then of course, most important of all is Dr Bion's work about vertices and his addendum to the model of the mind, his Grid and his theory of thinking; and then to see if I can tie these different directions together for the purpose of trying to investigate the central concept of symbol formation and its relationship to dreams and dream life. And if we have time, we might even get on to discuss the implications of all that for the theory of the psychoanalytical method and the psychoanalytical process and therapy.

---

1 A talk at the Psychoanalytic Center of California in 1979, with thanks to Jennifer Langham.

Now, I'm very addicted to history, and trying to understand the history of things, because language is a very misleading instrument, as you very well know; the same word can be used to mean entirely different things in different epochs of history and certainly, the same words have meant different things in different mouths in different epochs of psychoanalytic history. So it's almost always necessary to go back a bit and see how things developed.

Mind and brain

In a certain sense, the greatest difficulty that Freud met in the development of his model of the mind was in progressing from a very physiological and quantitative and hydrostatic model that grew out of the *Project for a Scientific Psychology* and libido theory, into the more truly psychological theory of the mind that is implied in the structural theory. Probably the greatest impediment that he met in coming to grips with the phenomena that he met in the consulting room was the problem of identification process, and this he met head on, you might say, in *Mourning and Melancholia*, where he found that he really couldn't describe – let alone explain – what happened to create this terrific confusion about who was really having the *pain* of melancholia. He could see quite clearly that the *pain* of mourning was in the mourner, and he could also see that pain of melancholia was somehow in everybody *around* the melancholic, but not in the melancholic himself; it's a great observation. But he found that he couldn't describe how this came about — was it the object that was in pain, because it was being maligned and ridiculed, or was the object causing pain to the ego – it got into a terrific muddle – and this seems to be the first time that he ran headlong into the problem of identification.

And second was the problem of masochism, where also he understood that there was some sort of identification going on, but he couldn't locate it, and he couldn't find the means of describing it. And even in that great paper 'A Child is Being Beaten', where he really pinpoints the problem of masochism, and through that the problem of sado-masochism and the complicated process of the perversions, he still isn't able to describe what is the structural situation that brings about this confusion of identity. He comes very close to it in some places: he describes, for instance, that a man may be identified with his penis in intercourse; or that he may be identified both with his penis and with the baby being beaten by that penis inside the woman, and so on.

But he really didn't have a concrete concept of the mind as separate from the brain and its neurophysiological apparatus, so couldn't find a language for describing and clarifying these processes. For this reason also, the concept of the mechanism of defence remained, in his hands, some mysterious neuro-mechanism which psychoanalysts could only assume existed, while he described the phenomena that were thrown up by the operation of these supposed neuro-mechanisms – repression being the prime example. He spent all his life trying to figure out how repression could come about.

Now it seems to me that when you read his work carefully, you can get some hint as to why or how it was that he came to this sort of impasse, where he couldn't make headway in discovering how different types of identification came about, although he was quite aware that there were different *types* of identification: that there were narcissistic identifications, and there was another type that was the heir to the Oedipus complex, and resulted in the establishment of a new institution in the mind, but he couldn't really find a language for describing it. There are two instances that stand out most clearly in *my* mind, that illustrate what it was *in* him that couldn't find a model that was sufficient to help him describe these things: one of them is in the Schreber case, where he describes the world destruction fantasy, and the destruction of Schreber's world. But he couldn't quite bring himself to describe it as an *internal* world. That is, a world that really existed inside his mind, although he *calls* it 'internal world'. But then he hedges it, and says, 'Oh well. It's really just the withdrawal of libido from object that caused these objects to disintegrate in Schreber's mind.'

An even earlier instance where you can see him balking at these more concrete descriptions, for instance in the Little Hans case, with that whole fascinating description by Hans, of what happened when he and his sister Anna used to ride in the stork box in the carriage, going to wherever it was it went. I mean, there a child told him exactly what children later told Mrs Klein of the phantasies of being inside the mother's body. But Freud couldn't take any interest in that, and as you remember, he treated it all as a sort of leg pull, in which Hans was having a kind of revenge on his father for telling him that the stork brought babies.

Now these sort of things seem to me very instructive: to understand that Freud was perhaps a man who was very bound to the outside world and very bound by his scientific and medical training to think of the mind as the brain, and couldn't quite separate himself from that. That is, he brought a very *sophisticated* mind to psychoanalysis, whereas Melanie Klein brought a very, in a sense, *naïve* mind to psychoanalysis. Although she'd begun medical studies and so on, she certainly had no real experience in the medical field, and was able to listen to children in a very naïve way, and to record what they told her; and what they started to tell her almost immediately was about these spaces. These spaces inside the body – inside the mother's body, and particularly inside their own bodies; the inhabitants of these spaces, and the importance of these spaces. And this she began to describe in her earliest papers on the development of a child, and subsequent papers, without, it seems to me, recognising that she was making a great leap in the psychoanalytic theory of the model of the mind.

This leap really changed the way of viewing the mind from a brain into a place – a place where thinking and feeling takes place, or just occurs. How it occurs, why it occurs, would be philosophical problems and not neurophysiological problems, according to this *level* of thinking about it. And of course, Dr Bion has come along with his Grid – he showed us very clearly that this is just one *level* for thinking about the mind. The concrete level is in a sense the *theological* level, where everything is told in narrative form, like the Bible: it is the truth of that level. So in a sense, the first move that Mrs Klein made in psychoanalysis was, to my mind, the most revolutionary move, but it was a very *quiet* move. Nobody noticed it, really. All they noticed at that time, and what all the squabbles were about in the British Society, was that she seemed to be saying that there were precursors of the superego that existed prior to the resolution of the Oedipus complex and the inception of the latency period. Terrible fights, that were essentially political fights, based on poor communication, took

place at that time. But the *real* revolution – that is, a new level
of formulation of the model of the mind that could be superimposed on Freud's structural theory of id, ego and super-ego
– *that* revolution really wasn't noticed.

Unconscious phantasy as mechanism of defence

It wasn't noticed, for instance, that this concrete way of representing the mind – as being made up of spaces that were occupied
by objects and parts of the self, both internal and external – lent
itself to a kind of theatrical exposition, an exposition in which
the concept of *phantasy*, and particularly *un*conscious phantasy,
came to replace the concept of the mechanism of defence. The
term was given a new meaning at a different level. This fact
wasn't recognised really until late in the '60s, after Mrs Klein's
death; and the most awful non-communication took place that
could easily have been resolved had this change in the model of
the mind been recognised at the time. That is, at this level of
theorising, the mechanism of defence *is* unconscious phantasy.

At Dr Bion's level, it changes again; it changes into lines –
we'll talk about that more later; it's an entirely different level of
abstraction. But at Mrs Klein's level, they are unconscious phantasies that really alter in a most concrete way the nature of the
object, the nature of the self, and the relationship between them,
especially in this great theatre of the inner world where meaning
is generated.

Of course, to say 'meaning is generated' one can easily forget
that psychoanalysis, up to that point was hardly concerned with
meaning. It was really concerned with conflicts of institutions of
the mental structure that Freud had elaborated in the structural
theory. The ego serving three masters, as he called it. It had nothing to do with the meaning of things. It only had to do, from
Freud's point of view, with the fact that these three institutions
of the superego, the id, and the outside world seemed to want
different things of the poor ego. And the poor ego had to play
them off against one another. It had nothing to do with the meaning of anything. But this revolution in the model of the mind,
that superimposed on Freud's model a concept of spaces and of a
theatre *inside* the mind where parts of the self and objects move

in … mythological dance, you might say – this brought meaning, and unconscious phantasy as an expression of meaning, into the forefront of psychoanalytic investigation in the consulting room. Now the concept of spaces is one which in a sense all of us who came, as it were, late into psychoanalysis from the '40s on – have grown up with, and rather take for granted. I think we often don't realise how difficult it is to get one's mind into a sufficiently naïve state to grasp the concreteness of this concept; because it is really a naïve concept – that is, a *childish* concept. It's about how children think; how the child in oneself thinks; and how the child in oneself thinks in dream pictures. And these dreams are about real things that are really happening inside the mind: real parts of oneself and real objects. And this word 'real', in reference to the internal situation, seems to me extremely difficult to get one's mind around in a truly emotional way.

Now this concept of spaces Mrs Klein described in passing, about children in the '20s. It first threw up the theory of the early precursors of the superego or early objects, partial objects, and the development of the whole-object relationships that then could approximate to Freud's description of the super-ego. The description of that could have come out of the work with children, without any reference at all to the concept of spaces inside the mind. And in a sense, that early work of hers, that raised so much of a storm, doesn't to my mind really belong to the great developments in psychoanalysis and its method and theory or model, because the concept of spaces only really began to bear specific fruit with the 1946 paper on schizoid mechanisms. And even there, in that paper, Mrs Klein herself rather hedges the question – although she had been talking now for 20 years about projection and introjection and internal objects and so on. When she came to talk about projective identification, that is, an omnipotent phantasy of a part of the self actually being insinuated, intruded into, projected into an object, she really only talked about it in relation to external objects.

And it seems to me that she herself had some difficulty in recognising the operation of projective identification with internal objects as a primary move in phantasy. Although she recognised that these objects in the outside world containing a projective identification, were then introjected, and that you ended up with an object inside containing a part of the self, and that this generated confusions of identity, hypochondria, claustrophobia, etc. She seemed, for some reason, reluctant to realise that the projective identification took place with internal objects initially, and not simply with external objects. You can see when you study the *Narrative* that even as late as the end of the 50s, she was a little reluctant to see projective identification as operating directly with internal objects. She'd been speaking of destructive attacks on objects by that time for 35 years. But her idea of sadistic attacks on objects was related mainly to oral and anal sadistic phantasy. And I think there was a certain reluctance in her to see the internal objects as *themselves* being vulnerable to this kind of intrusion.

In the *Narrative*, you can see it operating a bit in the portion in which she deals with Richard's little focus of paranoia about Cook and Bessie. There she's reluctant to recognise that the paranoia comes from the projection into Cook and Bessie – representing the breasts – of a really poisonous part of Richard, and it takes her the rest of the *Narrative* (of course, it's only another eight weeks) but still, it takes her the rest of it to work out that it was a poisonous part of Richard himself that really went into that object as an internal object and created in his own *inside* an object that could poison him – although he'd been having colds and pains in his tummy and so on, which she'd been interpreting to him all along.

I just mention that to illustrate that there is a tremendous emotional resistance that perhaps has to do with a fear of having a real persecutor, really inside your guts; and this (I *think*) plays a very important part in the resistance of people to recognising that such a thing as projective identification with an internal object is something that can occur in a moment, and that is particularly perhaps connected with masturbation practices and so on.

Now, I think, in a sense, that's about as far as Mrs Klein got with the development of a concept of space. She did evolve an addendum to the model of the mind that could be superimposed on Freud's, which changed the concept of internal world from a metaphor, or a bit of poetry, into a theoretical formulation that there was such a place inside the mind that really contained objects and parts of the self, and this opened up a whole field of exploration to her followers. And I would think that from 1946 until – well, with the exception of Dr Bion's work on thinking – you could quite well say that the work of her followers was more or less taken up with filling out this concept of projective identification, and of the internal world with its implications for the phenomenology of the consulting room.

Transference and countertransference

I would think that one of the first major technical and method-ological consequences erupted quite quickly after the 1946 paper and was stirred mainly by people in the British Society who had been deeply influenced by her work. These were the spurt of papers on countertransference: papers by Money-Kyrle, Paula Heimann, Margaret Little, Donald Winnicott.

Now, in order to understand why papers on countertransfer-ence should have blown up, and a technical advance should have resulted from her paper on projective identification, I think one has to go back and see that it was *that* paper in particular – the paper on projective identification – that made people realise that Mrs Klein had not only altered the concept of mechanism of defence and changed it into the concept of unconscious phantasy, but that in doing so, she had also altered the concept of transfer-ence. While in Freud's hands, transference was an expression of the repetition compulsion and a repetition of past events in the transference situation to the analyst; Mrs Klein transformed this into a concept of the externalisation of the internal situation onto the analyst, which therefore had an immediate implication. That is, the transference expressed in itself the patient's unconscious state of mind as represented by his infantile relationships to his internal objects and the identification processes that arose out of them. And that *this* is what was transferred into the outside world onto the analyst and manifest in the phenomenology of the consulting room.

This altered attitude towards the transference had the effect of opening the analyst's eyes to the ubiquity of transference phenomena. It wasn't enough to recognise that transference existed when the patient said, 'You remind me of my father'. It became apparent to people that the transference phenomena

–and a few years later they had to recognise also the countertransference phenomena – were existing in the room all the time, and that the analyst's task was to find them.

Of course, this was tremendously misunderstood when Mrs Klein talked about it in this way. She was immediately accused of saying, 'Everything is transference.' And she was immediately accused of *seeing* everything as transference. And I can remember, as late as 1975, having to get up in the British Society and say, 'No, that's not what she said. What she said was that everything has to be scrutinised to see if it gives evidence of the transference.' I suppose the truth is, if you *could* scrutinise everything carefully, you would find it in everything that goes on – but one isn't that skilful. However, that still isn't the same thing as saying that 'everything is transference', and it isn't the same thing – as she was earlier accused – as saying, 'children are psychotic'. Of course, she described the schizoid mechanisms, and equated them with some of the thought processes and so on that are seen *in* psychotics.

So that, in effect, seems to me to be where the picture of the development of the concept of spaces and its implications could be described as having been reached by the time of Mrs Klein's death in 1960. That she had, first of all, *created* this addendum to the model; she described for the first time the way in which narcissistic identifications can come about – at least one way in which they can come about by projective forms of identification. It had the consequence of altering the view of the transference, and therefore opened analysts' eyes to phenomena they hadn't previously looked at; and it brought in its wake this new interest in the countertransference as a *tool*, not just a nuisance.

Now, the explorations, particularly of the phenomena related to projective identification, that went on from 1946 on, and really are still going on, began to envisage a mental world that could be divided up into very specific spaces which seemed to have different laws governing the interaction in them, and different systems of meaning related to these interactions and the laws governing them.

And to try to give this some formal description: you may remember in the book *The Psychoanalytical Process* I describe this geography of the mind, trying to spell out the implications of Mrs Klein's model. That the mind could be envisaged as being contained in four different kinds of spaces: that is, the outside world, the world inside of external objects, the inside world, and the world *inside* internal objects; and I suggested at that time also that one had to consider that there was also a fifth space, the space of the delusional system whose essential quality was that it was *nowhere*. I'll just mention what seem to me to be the highlights of this exploration.

Herbert Rosenfeld made very important contributions in exploring and clarifying the way in which hypochondria comes about, through the operation of a system of double identifications. That is, that projective identification with a suffering internal object produces a very gripping type of identification because it has both projective and introjective aspects. And that seems to me to have been the major advance in the exploration of hypochondria. My own paper on anal masturbation demonstrated the way in which projective identification with internal objects can come about through masturbation practices that involve, particularly, the actual penetration of body orifices – mainly, anal penetration. Hanna Segal's paper on 'Depression in the schizophrenic' demonstrated the ways in which pain – mental pain – can be distributed through projective identification into external objects.

Narcissism

Herbert Rosenfeld began to describe narcissism in a way that was quite different from Freud's and in keeping with this new model of the mind of Mrs Klein's: described through what he called 'narcissistic organisations', instead of being a term for the distribution of the libido resulting in the muddle that Freud got into – having to call it 'narcissistic libido', and things of that sort. The narcissistic organisation underlying delinquency, the narcissistic organisation underlying perversion, and so on. The concept of narcissism has been given, through Mrs Klein's work, a new structural description: that is, of the relationship of infantile parts of the self to one another, as juxtaposed to their relationship to parental objects – part object or whole object. So, that concept of narcissistic organisation as a new way of describing narcissism, was brought into existence through the concept of spaces, and has led, again, to the recognition of the phenomenology of narcissism going beyond anything that Freud could have managed to describe, while narcissism was being used as a term referable to the term distribution and vicissitudes of the libido. It could have described that behaviour or symptomatology had a narcissistic basis but not how one part of the self could seduce, or threaten, or cajole another part into doing something that it fundamentally didn't want to do, that was hostile, and a betrayal to its good objects, and so on. If you're only talking on the basis of distribution of libido, you'd never be able, really, to describe these phenomena and their operations.

So the scope of psychoanalytic investigation was widened in these ways. Papers on drug addiction, on schizophrenia, manic depressive states, confusional states and so on, really crowded into the literature, partly stimulated also by Mrs Klein's later book on *Envy and Gratitude*, though that is not so much what I am talking about tonight – about the spaces.

Projective identification

Then finally, the concept of projective identification was transformed in Dr Bion's hands. Mrs Klein had viewed it really as fundamentally a pathological mechanism, an unconscious phantasy of pathological significance. Through Dr Bion it suddenly was transformed into something that could be seen as operative for a whole spectrum of purposes, from the most pathological (as in Hanna Segal's girl distributing her depressive anxiety with the flowers) to the most important developmental kind of activity as seen in the infant's communication with its mother: that is, as a primitive, prelingual means of communication for transmitting states of mind.

So the concept of projective identification, that was the first real fruit of the concept of spaces, has produced in turn this first break into a theory of thinking, and enabled Dr Bion to give, as you know, this *useful* description of the relationship of mother to baby, that has opened our eyes to a whole new level of phenomena in the consulting room: having to do with means of communication that go beyond the lexical use of language, to do with the music of language, the rhythm of language, the silences that fall, the inflections, and so on; and has *attuned* our ears to phenomena that simply passed over our heads previously.

Now, I think this isn't, by any means, the end of the investigation of projective identification – the usefulness of a concept of spaces is in many ways just dawning on us, you might say. And I thought this evening, I'd like to tell you about a most interesting case that we heard about in Italy, about two months ago. In order to illustrate for you this thesis that a space is a world, and that any world can be subdivided into sub-spaces, and each of these sub-spaces become a world that's governed by different laws and has different meaning and different significance. This is the world, inside the mother's body, that Mrs Klein began to describe very early, in her earliest work with children, and then formulated as the concept of projective identification; and this inside of the mother's body is a world that will lend itself to endless investigation in its relationship to psychopathology and the phenomena of the consulting room. And I'd like to tell you a little bit of clinical material that illustrates something about the specificity of the kind of hypochondriacal anxieties that result from a projective identification into different parts of the mother's body.

Subdivisions of the mother's body – clinical example

Now in a sort of theoretical, and you might say, *schematic* way, one finds continually the evidence that the inside of the mother's body is divided into general areas that have very specific phantasy and symptomatic and emotional significance; and these areas are generally divided through the waist, top and bottom, and divided front and back: mainly, top, front bottom and back bottom. And I want to tell you a bit about this clinical material that we heard in Perugia a couple of months ago, that I thought was quite marvellous.

It was about a boy of 17 who developed an acute psychotic episode in the middle of the main square in Perugia, stripped off his clothes, and disappeared down the sewer. And when they fished him out of there, he told them that he had done that to escape from Hitler, and essentially that Hitler was trying to enlist him to commit terrible, brutal acts of one sort or another.

During this period, while he was in the hospital, he wouldn't eat; he complained that the food smelled bad, thought it was poison; repeatedly escaped and left the hospital and had to be brought back. Although characteristically, he would elope from the hospital but then somehow find himself at a police station, or run into the police, and seemed to treat the police as fairly benevolent objects. During this time, psychoanalytic treatment was started, and he seemed to become very attached to his young woman analyst, but, as I remember it, during her holiday break, in the early months of his therapy, he again became panicky and eloped from the hospital and ended up in a mental hospital that, coincidentally, had the same name as his therapist, some hundred miles away.

Now, when he was brought back to the hospital, and started again in therapy, his complaint seemed to be very different. He was mainly worried about sexual assaults, mainly complaining about having sexual excitement projected into him. (He seemed to mistake the erotic excitement with his therapist.) And then he escaped from the hospital again, and when he was brought back this time, again, his symptomatology seemed to have changed. This time he was complaining that he was breathing too much, that the air seemed too rich for him and seemed to be enveloping him; that he was worried that he was taking too much of the air and there wouldn't be enough left for the other people in the hospital. He was particularly worried that he was hearing children crying, and felt that it was because they weren't getting enough air, and so on.

I can't remember much more of the detail, but that's enough to illustrate for you his migration around the inside of the mother's body, starting from getting into the sewer, up in her rectum, and being worried about being poisoned, and then getting into this hospital with the name of his woman therapist – that is, into the genital – and feeling terribly sexually excited, but also in danger of being sexually assaulted in there; escaping again, getting up inside the chest, and being enveloped by these – feeling he was a parasite inside the chest, taking up all the air, taking up all the oxygen, not leaving enough oxygen for the babies down in the womb who were felt to be crying and in need and so on.

So there, in brief, is an illustration of the minuteness, or you might say the precision with which the inside of the mother's body is sub-divided, and the specificity of the mental states that are thrown up by an experience of massive projective identification into different spaces, inside this particular space, inside himself – that is, inside the mother, inside himself – but also, in the transference, externalised onto his therapist, externalised onto the hospital, externalised onto the hospital that he got into that had the same name, and so on.

So this seems to me to be also one of the types of advance that comes from thinking of spaces in a very concrete way; it enables one to listen to clinical material in a way that you could not hear if you didn't have this kind of model: to think of the experience of living inside these spaces, and of encountering the kind of objects, the kind of substances, the kind of dangers, the kind of sensual experiences and so on, that the phantasy of those spaces includes.

Finally I want to stress that this whole theory of spaces – that is, in a sense, the whole Kleinian approach to psychoanalysis – is after all only one of many different lines of development and approaches, and has its particular strengths, and I suppose its particular weaknesses as well. This particular line of development, associated with Mrs Klein and her work, I think is correctly placed by Dr Bion in what he calls row C – that, is the mythology of the mind, the mind's mythology about itself, the level of mental functioning and the level of theories about mental functioning at which everything is metaphorical, and in which all experience is apprehended in narrative, dreamlike form, from which meaning is abstracted and raised to higher levels of abstraction from which verbalisation becomes possible, and so on, as Dr Bion's Grid described. It is therefore really, I think, correctly described as the theological level of operating in the consulting room. And I think it's a level that produces tremendously interesting types of analytic work. But as we go on in these lectures, I can also show you that it has its limitations as well, and that it is necessary, in order to cope with certain types of phenomena that we meet in our patients, to get beyond this theological level and this preoccupation with unconscious phantasy and try also to see the phenomena that relate to other aspects of mental functioning.

CHAPTER FOUR

Positive and negative forms[1]

(1970)

This is primarily a methodological paper insofar as its aim is to set out a problem in aesthetics, mainly related to sculpture and architecture, in a form that may lend itself to psychoanalytic solution, at a certain level, and then by some illustrations to draw forth a methodology to which analysts could, individually and collectively, contribute towards its investigation.

Let me try to state the problem first in a way that opens it, or at least some aspects of it, to psychoanalytic inquiry. Do spaces have formal qualities that are meaningful aesthetically, apart from the meaning of the objects by which they are bounded? The title of the paper is meant to suggest the question, put in another way: can we investigate spaces as negative forms?

I can launch immediately into a psychoanalytic elaboration of the problem by laying out in extended form the term 'space' as it is used in a technical sense, and for this purpose I would enumerate five potential spaces in the geography of the mind which may become actual, in the sense of the concreteness of psychic

---

1 Written 1970; first published in *Sincerity: Collected Papers of Donald Meltzer,* ed. A. Hahn (Karnac, 1994).

reality during personality development, healthy or pathological. Starting from inside out, I would list them as follows:

1) The space inside internal objects;

2) the space of internal reality;

3) the outside world;

4) the space inside external objects; and possibly (4a) , though I have seen no convincing evidence of its existence, the space inside the internal objects of external objects;

5) the world of schizophrenia, beyond the boundaries of the emotional gravitation of the breast and its system.

To return to 4(a), my doubt is not about its potential existence, but about its actual existence in the system of object relations which we study in the consulting-room. But from the point of view of the geography of phantasy, history is of this 'Russian doll' configuration, or like the folksong of the 'Old Woman who Swallowed a Fly' ('cider inside her inside'). This applies to both past and future, for just as the internal mother contains her mother containing her mother, etc., she also contains her babies containing their babies, etc. This I feel to be a very important point, for it reminds us that in moving from category to category of our roster of 'spaces', we are also journeying in time, not in its chronometric sense, but in its categorial sense: past, present, future.

Now let us turn to some clinical examples, after which I can return to methodological considerations.

Clinical examples

Example A

A girl of fourteen, whose analysis had carried her from early latency in the playroom to the flux of puberty on the coach, dreamed that *five criminals were imprisoned in a flimsy slatted structure high in a tree, but each night they escaped and roamed abroad in the village. Then she was one of them and they were in Regents Park, but it was in the time of Charles II.*

This dream relates to long-standing nocturnal masturbatory games and phantasies in which fingers were personified and engaged in various dramas in relation to the surfaces and orifices of her body. The spaces of interest are the slatted prison up in the tree and the round Regents Park.

Example B

A young married man whose wife was thought pregnant for the first time had the following dream: *She was peeping into the window of an office building and could see a room with a purple stripe round the walls, decorated with small golden eagles. Leading in from the main entrance was a hundred-foot-tall passage called 'Nelson's cabin'.*

The spaces of interest are the eagles' room (uterus) and 'Nelson's cabin', built to receive Nelson's column (Nelson being in assonance with Meltzer), i.e. the vagina.

Example C

A married young woman who started her analysis after a one-year interruption (her previous analysis gradually falling apart after the death of both her parents within a short period of time) dreamt that *she was one of two students who were running around to avoid being expelled from a building that looked like the Albert Hall or a Cathedral, and was filled with people sitting in rows of benches. From the top of a central structure a man was conducting what seemed to be a combination of religious ceremony and a stormy Union meeting; the public shouted out their demands, and the man responded from the pulpit.*

The space is the inside of the breast swarming with babies and presided over by the central penis-nipple. This compares with the structure of the Pantheon with its open dome and its central open space, or with St Peter's dome with Michelangelo's canopy beneath it.

Example D

A young unmarried man in his third year of analysis had made noticeable progress regarding his confusional states, his periods of apathy and sexual immaturity. But he always found it discouraging at weekends and holidays when his dependence on the analytic breast gradually took the place of his usual delusional independence based on his intellectual superiority and his personal fortune. The patient was having a whole series of dreams in which the breasts were represented in an architectural way as domes, tents, windmills, etc. One week, on Wednesday and Friday, he had two dreams of this type, in which he showed his reluctance to give up his omnipotent intrusion into the breast.

Wednesday: *He was in the ring of a circus tent standing on a slatted structure which suddenly began to spiral up like an escalator carrying him towards an apex, very frightened of falling.*

Friday: *He was on the street outside a structure like those used for advertising posters in Paris. It seemed to be the Communist Party headquarters and a man was entering with his small son. When the door opened it looked very warm and snug inside and the patient realised how cold he was outside.*

On the Thursday he had brought a dream whose significance I did not comprehend until the Friday dream had suggested that the dreams of the three days could be arranged together spatially:

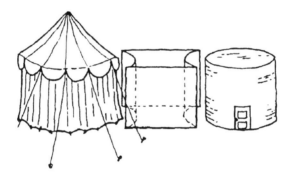

He had dreamed that he was in a rectangular room, or rather its two ends bulged inward as a convexity. In the centre was a swimming pool, which looked black, he thought, until he noticed that there was no roof and only the night sky was above. The analyst's voice was then heard saying that it might seem lonely at first, but he would quite like it once he was accustomed to it.

This dream seems to represent as a space the period of waiting, with the memory of having been lifted to the breast and the prospect of its repetition, i.e. the linear structure of past-present-future.

These examples are given in barest outline, merely to illustrate the categories of spaces and their relationship to the conceptualisation of time as a dimension of life space which is represented so concretely in unconscious phantasy.

Before we turn now to methodological considerations, I would like to give a further example from a different class of analytic data.

Example E

A student of architecture, the younger of two children, had been in analysis for some five years when, as part of his training programme, he was asked to design a nursery school. At that time his analysis was blanketed by an acting-out with a girlfriend, which completely recapitulated the secret sexual relationship to an older sister during early childhood, in which they had dramatised their appropriation of sexuality from parents whose marriage was coming adrift.

In keeping with the severe resistance that dominated his analysis, material referable to the project did not enter until it had been completed and rejected by his teachers as being more suitable for a prison than a nursery school. He had designed a single large, high room, surrounded by a catwalk onto which the front entrance opened at street level, and from which a ramp descended into the room, which opened upon an outdoor play area with a pool and surrounded by high, unadorned brick walls. In short, he had designed an interior for the mother's body in which babies were eaten, cast into the rectum, and defaecated into the toilet.

Methodology

The methodological aspect of this paper falls into two sections: 1) the requirements for analytic research into aesthetic problems in this area, and 2) the formulation of problems for investigation.

Material of value in this area is almost exclusively derived from the analysis of adult patients and is of three sorts:

1) patients' description of the spaces in which they live in the outside world;

2) dreams;

3) spaces patients create in the course of creative work.

If accurate information is to be gathered regarding the formal aspects of these spaces, inquiry by the analyst is often necessary, and must be carried on systematically as part of his technique, as retrospective inquiry is extremely unreliable.

The significance of specific spatial configurations can only be reliably defined by those that appear in series and not by isolated instances.

The significance must be derived from the transference and not from speculation. It is useless to define a space as 'vagina', or 'inside the breast', as these are mere notational terms and tell nothing about the individual meaning.

Only when spatial forms are identified in series in an individual and found to be akin in a series of cases, can any statement useful to the aesthetician be made by the psychoanalytic investigator.

This last point brings us to the second section of the methodology: namely, the formulation of the problem. Insofar as these are problems of aesthetics, we can assume that psychoanalysts are not likely to be in a position to formulate the problem at all. However, a student of aesthetics wishing to have a problem investigated could ask for it to be circulated to psychoanalysts for inquiry and await the results. To such research ends, a clinical data service has been inaugurated among some 85 Kleinian analysts of thirteen countries, to which people are invited to submit problems of applied psychoanalysis for collective probing.

CHAPTER FIVE

The aesthetic object[1]

(1984)

Some will have noticed that I speak more and more often of 'aesthetic objects'. It is true that in my analytical practice certain changes have occurred with regard to my ideas on the nature of psychic suffering, and the organisation of the defensive processes against this suffering. These ideas deviate somewhat from those of Melanie Klein. This is partly due to the gradual assimilation of Dr Bion's ideas on what he calls the caesura of birth – the transition from being an aquatic to air-breathing animal. We can focus on this transition. We can start thinking about intrauterine life, at least in the last months of it, as a period when the child will have emotional experiences. From what the clinical material shows us, we can attempt to conceptually grasp the nature of this experience, as well as the way in which it prepares the child for the transition to a life outside the maternal body. We can take into consideration something of the order of instinctual preparation, or, as Bion would say, innate preconceptions which are already in the process of being established in utero: the different sensory

---

1 Talk given to the GERPEN in 1984; published in *Meltzer à Paris*, ed. J. Touzé (Hublot, 2013). Retranslated into English from the French.

devices (visual, auditory, gustatory, etc.) are already stimulated by the nature of the environmental object in which the baby is dimly contained. We can also take into account the fact that, during the last two months of intrauterine life, the baby begins to be very constrained by this container; he has now almost no room to move. He can, of course, move and change position, but, in my opinion, he must feel terribly stuck in there; his body must aspire towards freeing himself from this constriction. It seems to me that Bion was absolutely right to think that the foetus is not aware of its growth; it is much more likely that it feels that the claustrum is shrinking around it, as seen in some dreams.

So if you think about this final month in which the various senses are ready to work but receive only very hazy stimuli, where the muscles and the body are also ready to work but cannot do so in this terrible state of constriction, release from this prison must have the emotional significance of freedom – the freedom to function. Various clinical experiences have strongly suggested to me that this exit from the tunnel, this explosion of the senses that occurs with the appearance of the outside world, must constitute the first aesthetic experience. I am thinking for example of certain dreams of patients, or of certain children at the beginning of their therapy whose development does not seem to get going until they find a therapist paying the kind of attention that is then reciprocated by a real explosion of love towards the object.

The clinical material that we heard yesterday illustrates quite what Melanie Klein described concerning the oscillation between the paranoid-schizoid and depressive positions; however, this material can also be described as the oscillation between part-object and whole object, or between a quantitative and qualitative relation to the world, or between absence and presence of meaning, or even, between absence and presence of emotion. All these different aspects are implied in the distinction between paranoid-schizoid position and depressive positions.

As a result of such clinical situations, I am increasingly inclined to think that it is not useful to think of the infant as having equipment so immature that he can have only very primitive emotional experiences. Anyway, there has to be a starting point.

It doesn't seem useful to say that emotional experiences start at the age of four, or four months, or four days, or four days before birth. At some point there is an emotional impact of the world on the self. From the internal point of view, and bearing in mind the model of a traumatic escape from a claustrum, we can also imagine escaping from a two-dimensional, automatised life of causality, where things are only what they seem to be and nothing else: escaping to another world of experience whose imperative consists in the emotions awakened in the subject by the beauty of the world.

It seems to me that, until we have been dazzled by the beauty of the object, the question of whether it is as beautiful inside as outside, does not occur. This question constitutes, in my view, the very heart of what we mean by meaning. This corresponds very well to what Melanie Klein called the epistemophilic drive, the first object of which is the interior of the mother's body (today also understood as the interior of her psyche: what she thinks, what she feels, her intentions, her story, etc.). If we make the link with Dr Bion's model of the thinking apparatus, in particular the alpha-function that serves to think thoughts, the stimulus to form thoughts would be the arousal of the question 'But is it beautiful inside?' The need to ask this question leads to alpha-function, the formation of symbols, dream-thought, etc.

It seems to me that it makes a big difference in your clinical approach if you think in these terms: that is, if you think of the paranoid-schizoid position not as primitive, but as the position to which one withdraws to protect oneself against the impact of the beauty of the object, against emotionality, against the problems and questions that this impact raises. The paranoid-schizoid position is a defensive position, it is always a defence against the pain of the depressive position.

This question, is it beautiful inside? is the essence of the depressive position. And it seems to me that this has important repercussions in our way of working. If you think of the paranoid-schizoid position as the first developmental position, leading on to the depressive position, you will pay very close attention to the phenomenology of the paranoid-schizoid position and all its detailed processes of cleavage, projective identification, etc., thinking that in this way, quite naturally, the transference will evolve.

But if, on the contrary, you think that the first developmental experience is the explosive experience of the beauty of the object, with the question 'Is it as beautiful inside?' marking the source of confusion, then your attention will always be focused on looking for signs of the impact of aesthetic objects, as well as the defences against this impact. You will observe your material in a very different way. In addition, it seems to me that if you follow material of a paranoid-schizoid nature by showing a great interest in its details, this will have the effect of giving this level of phenomenology a respectable status, as well as a tendency to prolong its existence. It is almost a perversion of analysis. Significant attention paid to the details of a patient's perverse sexual activities – to the small details of his obsessive activities, or to the rational concoctions of his paranoid ideas, etc. – almost constitutes a secret complicity with the patient in remaining ignorant of the depressive phenomena.

But this requires certain conditions in the analyst himself, in terms of his vision of the world. Because you can only adopt this position of aesthetic focus if you consider that it is the only rational position that one can adopt *vis-à-vis* life, and *vis-à-vis* the world. If you are too impressed with what you read in the newspapers, if you think that these represent well what life is on our planet, it will be impossible for you to adopt this position with your patients. Inevitably, sooner or later, you will have a more pessimistic view of the world. But if, instead of reading the newspapers, you go for a walk in the countryside, or to the Jeu de Paume, or if you read Shakespeare, etc., you will have a completely different impression, and you will see that the question which embraces everything which concerns us is: 'Ah! But is it as beautiful inside?'

Question: In this wide picture, what place do you give to what Mrs Esther Bick has described of the baby's intense search for identity by adhesive means in the first weeks or first months of life?

Donald Meltzer: It seems to me that adhesive identification, two-dimensionality, group mentality, the 'second skin' personality as Mrs Bick calls it, or what Dr Bion calls the invertebrate personality, are different aspects of withdrawal into the paranoid-schizoid position; but these are very severe withdrawals, which go beyond that of the cleavage processes and projective identification mechanisms described by Melanie Klein in 'Notes on some schizoid mechanisms' (1946). In this paranoid-schizoid defence system, the crucial step is the one that reduces the symbol to the sign: that is, it is a mechanism which leads to treating the symbols born from the dream processes as simple referential signs of objects from the outside world, rather than seeing them as mysterious objects in themselves, that need to be explored in order to extract the meaning.

This sign-language is the essential step in withdrawing from a depressive mentality into a paranoid-schizoid mentality. Symbols are used as if they were only signs: a = b and therefore b = a, nothing mysterious about it. For the making of signs is only a conventional method for representing one thing by another; but the creation of a symbol is an entirely different process – the breast and the mountain cannot be exchanged for one another as representations. A symbol brings them together and creates a third object, a new object called mountain-breast or breast-mountain, and you can descend into this mine-pit that is thought, to extract the ore that is meaning. There is probably a difference depending on whether it is mountain-breast or breast-mountain, that is to say, at times you will be tempted to try to understand why mountains have an emotional impact so important to you, and you will then explore the mountains; at other times, a woman's breasts will have such an impact, and then you will examine the mountain-breasts. This is the essence of what Bion calls the use of reversible perspective as a method of investigating and testing reality.

CHAPTER SIX

The evolution of object relations[1]

(1997)

First of all, that's what I call a hard act to follow[2] – the word from the Castle making us all feel peasants down in the courtyard. What I want to speak about is first of all to tell you my thoughts on material from observation and clinical analysis. Then I want to talk about what – you might say pretentiously – I would call the sociology of genius, the situation which Bion himself has written about, and the position of the genius in the group, and with some ideas about the internal life of the genius as well.

To start with some material, just to give you something in the back of your mind that has to do with what has been called the origin of object relations – but is really the origin of confusion about objects. There are three bits of material. Two of them are from seminars in Venice.

The first was an observation of a child and her mother – an eighteen-month-old child who was living with a mother whose husband had deserted her. The two of them were in a rather bad state of absolute adhesiveness to one another that prevented both

---

1 First published in the *British Journal of Psychotherapy*, 14(1): 60-66 (1997).
2 The previous paper at the conference, by Parthenope Bion Talamo.

of them from eating and they were getting emaciated. A very, I think, talented social worker was called in who functioned simply as an observer, hardly saying a word but tolerating the clingingness of both child and mother, observing their interaction and trying to understand it. Over a period of six months the introduction of a third person into this adhesive relationship significantly altered things so that both child and mother began to manifest mental processes and not simply this adhesiveness that seemed to be devoid of phantasy and devoid of emotions And their feeding improved as well. The child began to play, began to exhibit naughtiness. The mother began to have emotions towards the child and so on. It seemed to be accomplished simply by being there as an interested and thoughtful observer, observing this adhesiveness and its mindlessness.

The second piece of material from the same seminar was a report of a preliminary interview with a seven-and-a-half-year-old boy who was thought to be autistic, who was unable to speak. But he wasn't terribly troublesome or manifesting great disturbance – he just seemed to be ineducable. During an hour's interview he didn't play. The interviewer tried to interest him in various things and the boy seemed to get irritable towards him. Then, touching upon his experience at school, he asked the boy whether they did any music at school. The boy brightened up and said 'Yes', and went to the blackboard and drew what strongly resembled a stave of notes of music. He couldn't sing it but the pictorial representation of it seemed to please him. Then he said to the observer 'Now look what happens', and he then drew on the blackboard what was obviously a cloud. This seemed to bring him to life. This cloud also had attached to it another little cloud of rather equally nebulous shape. Then he rubbed it out and again drew a cloud and a second cloud, and this second cloud clearly had the shape of a heart – the conventional shape of a heart – and he said 'Now watch what happens'. Now a third cloud appeared and this third cloud began to emit bolts of lightning towards the little heart-shaped cloud. With some excitement the little boy drew the turning back of these bolts of lightning so that they were turned back against this third cloud. Then the lightning was erased and the little cloud itself was erased and he said 'Now the first cloud eats up this

third cloud.' Then there appeared inside the first cloud a reoc-
currence of this heart-shaped cloud – now quite clearly in the
form of a baby.

That sort of nebulousness and the evolution of nebulousness
is the subject that came up in the discussion of Parthenope Bion's
paper in a question about the triadic relationship and its contribution to the capacity for thought. And this seemed to be an
illustration of the impingement on the dyad of the third partner.
It certainly indicated this little boy was thinking and was able to
make a remarkable representation of what he was thinking about.

Now to come to a bit of material from a patient of mine who
has been with me for about four years – a very difficult lady of
whom one can be fond only if you are fond of fighting, because
she is very pugnacious. The first compliment she ever paid me
was to say 'Well, I can see at least you have got guts.' For the four
years it has continued with that sort of swordplay, hoping not to
be wounded and trying not to wound her. There were various
turning points. She began to bring dreams and got to be quite
a good dream-rememberer. Some of them were very interesting
dreams and they constituted various watersheds in the evolution
of the transference. But the transference remained entirely this
combat with the man, a paranoid attitude towards men, their
aggressiveness, their subduing of women, and representations of
this in the community and so on.

I want to tell you about three dreams that seem to me to
constitute a watershed of really finding a new level in the transference. These three dreams came after a period of about six months
in which there was a very noticeable change in the atmosphere of
the consulting room. That is, to every session she came in like a
lion but from most of the sessions she went out like a lamb and it
wasn't clear what brought about these transitions.

At the Christmas break, to my astonishment, she organised
herself to go to Italy, to Florence and Siena. Now, in my consulting
room there are two posters as a grudging surrender to decoration.
One is about a yard long and about six inches high, positioned
over the couch, and is a representation of the *Horseman of Siena*
by Simoni Martini. Across the room over the desk is a quite large
poster that says at the bottom of it 'Firenze' and is a detail from
Uccello's *Battle of San Romano*. So this trip to Italy, which was the

first happy holiday that she had had, perhaps ever in her life but certainly in the course of the analysis, became known between us as 'life on the Firenze–Siena axis'. She accepted this as having to do with life in the consulting room and particularly with the sessions when she became like a lamb.

Now, the three dreams that I wanted to tell you. In the first of them *she was on a bus trip, a group bus trip. As they went along there seemed to be a second bus – or really a first bus – that was ahead of them and there was something very beautiful. She couldn't quite tell whether it was the colour of this first bus that was so beautiful, or was it a landscape against which she was seeing the bus. But then suddenly both buses had a tyre blow out and had to stop, and people had to file off the buses while the tyre was being repaired – or replaced. As she was walking out of her bus she kissed the driver, whom she didn't know. But as she kissed him she got a very strong taste, or smell, it wasn't clear, of fruit pie in her mouth, in her nose.* That was the first dream. I thought to myself, 'Well, there is something beautiful about, and it certainly looks like the breast, but nipple and penis very confused'. And this seemed to be borne out in the second dream.

In the second dream *she was sitting in an auditorium waiting for a lecture. She was sitting on a seat that was like a seat on an aeroplane that could be tipped far back, and she tipped her seat far back so that she was practically lying in the lap of the man behind her, whom she knew faintly and knew that he had a rather ugly name which I couldn't remember. In this position, almost lying on his lap, she was nuzzling his arm which was hairless and it was definitely pleasant.* That was the second dream, both of which occurred in the same week.

The third dream, which I must admit delighted me, was that *she was a baby and she was lying in her cot playing with her feet – with her feet in the air and playing with her toes. Then she thinks she had an orgasm and the room levitated and began travelling slowly through the air. And as it travelled through the air she saw out of the window the dome of the Duomo in Florence, and was struck by the beauty of the red tiles.* So I thought to myself, 'Well, it isn't that she has found the breast and nipple in her mouth but she has discovered the other breast and it won't be long before she discovers the one that's in her mouth, if she can see the beauty of the other breast'.

Now the problem which I linked to the little boy's drawings of the cloud, which I think has so much to do with the overcoming of adhesiveness between mother and baby. This nebulousness of the object seems to be something that Bion has touched on – I can't remember exactly where – but it certainly is contained in the 14th century religious tract, *The Cloud of Unknowing*. 'The most godly knowing of God is that which is known by unknowing.' The author calls this book *The Cloud of Unknowing* because of the same conviction that God is to be attained in this life, in the highest way that He may be obtained, not by way of knowledge but by way of ignorance. Of course I am sure Bion knew this tract and has more or less quoted it – it is not only Keats that he is quoting about negative capability.

So what this little boy has drawn would seem to me to be worthy of the description of the evolution of the cloud of unknowing, changing first into the possibility cloud with the heart-shaped baby cloud attached to it; and then the emergence of the oedipal situation and the turning back of the lightning; and then the one cloud eating up the other cloud, and its appearing then as a baby inside the first cloud. I think we can say that this is the evolution to a cloud of possibility – that is, the movement from the cloud of unknowing to the cloud of possibility and then, with the emergence of the baby inside, the cloud of probability.

It seems to me that most people do not get beyond this third stage of evolution of objects – in which the nebulousness begins to take on form and then begins to acquire function as well, and this wedding of form and function begins to produce the experience of beauty in the object.

As I say, this step in the delineation of objects, that starts with this cloud of unknowing, and becomes a possibility and then a probability, does produce a sense of knowing. The closest we get to God is only in the stage of the cloud of unknowing that has neither form nor function. Bion has said things very much like that in the voice of his character Priest in the third book of the *Memoir*. When scientific knowledge and spiritual unknowing are compared there is great uncertainty as to which is the more valuable. What I want to propose to you is that the evolution of objects from cloud of unknowing to possibility to probability *is* the scientific route, and is as close as the peasants down in the courtyard ever get to knowledge. Bion is a slightly different animal, meaning that not only does he have the drive for knowledge (which is, for instance, illustrated in the determination which he could bring to bear on things) but he also has an amazing complexity and penetration of mind which – once he discovered these ways of liberating his mind to function (which includes, of course, eschewing memory and desire, and setting his mind free to observe and think) – does manifest a level of mental functioning that, I think, most of us absolutely cannot follow.

Of course, Parthenope Bion's paper, which does follow his concepts chronologically and – I think – accurately and rather beautifully, must not be mistaken for getting into Bion's mind and really knowing what Bion thought and felt. Because I think with this level of mental function that we call genius there are qualities that either sweep you along or leave you far behind – one or the other. When they sweep you along this does tend to generate around the genius a particular atmosphere of elitism which eventually becomes a cage and a trap for him, which he feels impelled to escape and liberate himself from. The great example of this is Ludwig Wittgenstein, who generated at Cambridge such an atmosphere of elitism and such a penumbra of hatred around him that he did escape from it and went first to Austria and built a house for his sister, and then he went to the mountains to teach in a school, which was almost a disaster. Finally he went back to Cambridge in a very altered state of mind and with a very altered message from the one that he had employed in writing the *Tractatus* (1922); he began to explore language in an entirely different way – not defining, not calculating, not laying down the law but simply inspecting and observing and thinking – and produced a quite readable book, *Philosophical Investigations* (1953). Francesca Bion will correct me but I think Bion also fled from the adulation in London, which not only was an umbra of adulation but had a penumbra of hatred and contempt around it which was not comfortable. He fled to California, which I think was also something of a disaster for him, although it enabled him to alter his method and also to produce his trilogy (*A Memoir of the Future*) – what he jokingly called, Francesca Bion says, a pornographic novel. It is full of his humour (wry as it is) and really is not a bit pornographic except for some dirty words (which are always to the point). I suspect Mrs Klein had some similar flight from adulation and contempt and finally settled down and wrote *Narrative of a Child Analysis*, which to my mind – I may be unjust – seems to be the greatest unread book in psychoanalysis.

Of course this process in Bion had an interesting point in which he, it seems to me, sort of savaged himself in *Second Thoughts* (1967). But he wasn't savaging only himself. He was savaging the whole of psychoanalysis about its failure to find a language which was comprehensible and precise. And when Parthenope Bion says that he was working on the edge of language, it was on the same edge that Wittgenstein was working – the limits of language: the limits of what can be said and what has to be shown, and the way in which what has to be shown is either graphic or musical, or the combination of words and music which is poetry. And certainly what is so enduring in Bion's work is this poetry. Unfortunately, of course, the poetry lends itself to apostolic translations and reconstructions. Bion, I think, at a moment in *The Dawn of Oblivio*n (1979) says that at first his thoughts were treated as incomprehensible, but after a period of time they seemed to become so comprehensible that they were considered to be commonsense. But later, of course, he was accused of plagiarism as people thought that he had stolen his commonsense ideas from them.

This is a fairly common phenomenon in analysis. This lady of the flying dome of Florence is a great one for paraphrasing an interpretation which then turns up in the next session as her own thought; and she is capable of greeting an interpretation with the immediate 'Well, I have always known that'; and of course she accuses me of robbing her mind in order to give lectures and write books that she is really writing. So this phenomenon that Bion reports is really a fairly common phenomenon in analysis, in this difficult problem of trying to find a language, because sitting behind a patient one is not in a very strategic position for showing what can't be said.

Of course, language isn't all you use in psychoanalysis; there is the music of the voice. And I think in the earlier years of analysis it is probably much more the music of the voice, and what it conveys of the countertransference, that has some therapeutic effect. At least, it moves the transference on and one sort of trusts that this is therapeutic. But the attempts to avoid action in favour of communication are very, very difficult and probably impossible. Everything you say or do in analysis also has a component of action in it. One of the things about the grid which I think Bion really corrected in his *Memoir of the Future*, particularly in the third volume, *The Dawn of Oblivion*, was that it was probably a mistake to put action in column six, as the endpoint of thought (very much like the way precipitation in a chemical experiment is the endpoint of that particular chemical reaction), because it is the endpoint, because action does put a stop to the thought. When he says, quoting Poincaré, that the answer is the misfortune of the question it is because the answer is a conversation-stopper – it does announce and explain, and puts an end to thought and is an action. It, following my little boy's cloud formations, the question with its cloud of unknowing doesn't mature into a possibility cloud and then into the probability cloud with a baby inside (the baby being the next question), if it doesn't give birth to the next question, it has been aborted, really – it has been stopped in its tracks.

Of course, I do think that Bion got fed up with all of us in London. I think to myself: 'Well, he didn't really get fed up with me', because – unlike what Robin Anderson says – I didn't work closely with him; I didn't have supervision with him or analysis with him. In some way, you might say, I managed to remain on friendly terms with him – mainly by not doing too much with him. I think he did get fed up with the London scene, which I see as an imprisonment by not a cloud of unknowing but a cloud of knowing. And that is the elitism – this cloud of knowing what Bion meant.

After writing the portion of *The Kleinian Development* on Bion's work (1978), the outcome of it was that I was pretty sure that I didn't understand him and that no amount of study was going to improve that situation, that I must find some way of enjoying him. It seemed to me that the way to enjoy Bion was very much what he himself had advised: just read it; don't try to understand it, don't try to figure it out; just read it, enjoy it and if you are lucky you will be inspired by it. That certainly seems to me to be the case. The best I can hope is that these cloudy unknowing objects will have some sort of struggle with one another – like this lightning business – or that they will have some sort of intercourse with one another and produce babies. But I am at best the container of these objects and I do best to let them have a life of their own. That seems to me to be what Mrs Klein came to in the notes to *Narrative of a Child Analysis*, in which I think she at last declared her liberation from Freud – or from the Freudian model, the Freudian mechanics, the Freudian reliance on quantities and so on. As to *A Memoir of the Future* I think Bion also has liberated himself – not just from Freud but from Mrs Klein as well: liberated himself and of course liberating his sense of humour and his perspective, the vertex from which he sees himself. *The Dawn of Oblivion* ends with a marvellous seminar in which a pretty fair cross-section of the human personality is represented, in conflict and affection toward one another, in a way that is pretty impressive and tremendously interesting. All the things that were dealt with in those wonderful first papers, and in *Learning from Experience*, and finally in *Attention and Interpretation* (1970), are covered in these three volumes. I think it is not unreasonable to say it was his masterpiece.

Of course, it brings up the whole question about loyalty and the sociological – the social function of loyalty which doesn't mean anything except an idealisation of mindlessness ('My country right or wrong'; Bion right or wrong; Mrs Klein right or wrong; Freud right or wrong). That is not the same as the acceptance of the cloud of unknowing. It is of interest, in the Old Testament, that the only person who ever gets a sight of God is Moses – and he is only allowed to see a sort of passing moment as God's backside disappears ...

That is the position of the child in relation to these internal parents: as far as really seeing them and seeing them with anything other than this nebulousness, it just doesn't happen. The clearest view we ever get of the internal parents is in our dreams. My patient's dream of the dome of the Duomo is the clearest sight she will ever have of the internal mother's breast and its beauty, and its meaning to her. It is on this 'Siena–Firenze' axis, which of course is keeping the father's penis at least a few hundred kilometres away from the mother's breast, which is about the state she is in at present – that she can tolerate the idea of the mother's breast, and its meaning to her, so long as she can keep this attractive penis at a distance, the one that she was nuzzling in the seat behind her, the one that she kissed and that tasted like fruit pie and so on. That is the best she can do at the moment. But it is a tremendous advance for her, and one that has relieved me to such an extent that I actually have had a letter from her apologising for being beastly in yesterday's session – quite touching, delivered by hand.

The question comes up, and is raised by Bion in the *Memoir,* of what is this business about progress? What do we mean when we say a patient is making progress? I have expressed my opinion about that in *The Apprehension of Beauty* (1988), and I think it is borne out in the sort of material I have just talked about. The caesura of birth, as Bion says, is not a caesura from being a primitive animal to being a human being – it is a caesura in the intensity of impact, as the baby in the womb has plenty of experience and plenty to think about. But what it doesn't have is the beauty of the world. That only impinges on him as he emerges from his mother's womb. Its impact, I think, is pretty powerful. Not immediately perhaps, not while the experience is just the two-body, dyadic relationship, but as soon as the father with his lightning-penis enters and there is the sense of conflict and combat that the beauty of the object (and the beauty of the capacity to apprehend the object) is felt sensually, as a sensual mode. And as a sensual mode it is by its intensity intolerable to most children – not to all children, but to most children. There certainly are children whose capacity for aesthetic impact is abnormally great. Perhaps this is the key to genius: the capacity to tolerate aesthetic impact; an abnormal responsiveness to the aesthetic of the object and the aesthetic of the world and therefore, of course, an abnormally intense response to the vandalising of it.

CHAPTER SEVEN

A reverie on the baby's interior preoccupation[1]

(2002)

Aprofessional and personal experience gradually distills into something precise and intelligible that can be put on paper. It relates to observation of the baby after feeding but before being overtaken by sleep when his sense of self has withdrawn behind his skin to the busy world of his internal organs with their borborygmi and shifting tensions. The child is alone with himself, feeling the encapsulated warmth of his body, the various rhythms of breathing, pulse, the gastro-intestinal movements, the amazing well-being of his internal chemistry and the incipient bound of his vitality. Above all there is the vague sense of growth going on in its mysterious quietness. All this is the screen for his attention.

But its diffuseness gradually focuses on the fate of the food he has taken in and the processes that will eventuate in evacuation. But for the baby it is an enthralling process, fraught with uncertainty and struggle: to digest, to resist the impulse to vomiting, to separate the gas bubble from the pain it engenders, to accept the isolation of the internal struggle without calling out

---

1 Written c.2002 for the Psychoanalytic Group of Barcelona; part published in *A Meltzer Reader* (Harris Meltzer Trust, 2010)..

for help, knowing there is no help available for he is alone with these processes and his ignorance. In brief I am trying to imagine the dawn of imagination and the baby's evidences for thought. His experience is vague, fluid except for its polarity – the feed that starts the process and the evacuation that brings a sense of relief, of completion, and a mysterious sense of purpose fulfilled.

What I am describing could be called the birth of meaning. In all of these processes the baby feels helpless, passive toward his organs and their functions. But the polarizing of his awareness finds a use for his surging vitality in the form of resisting the organs' rebelliousness and constraining their ignorance. I am trying to envisage the galvanising of attention, the birth of imagination, the excitement of incipient meaning and eventually of purpose. Therefore the possibility of fatigue and relaxation, but also of success or failure. This is an attempt to formulate a metapsychology of the neonate (its aloneness between feeds, ignorance of the mother's mentality, schooled only by the rhythm of her services, unable to form symbols and have meaningful dreams, bound to sensation, at best anecdotal in recollection, not even linear, on the verge of chaos). It is not surprising if it comes out sounding like Genesis. In the beginning was the feed. What we are relying on is this galvanising of intelligence by attention to the polarity, for it is not in the beginning was the formless infinite but the placenta as the primary feeding object. We might call this the experience of *surprise* and rewrite our genesis as a process starting with birth and panic relieved by surprise, not only surprise at finding the breast but surprise at an extraneous intelligence, the beginning of revealed religion. All the functions described are the fruits of identification with the extraneous intelligence. In the beginning object relations and identification are simultaneous (Freud).

At this point in our conjecture we have a baby surprised to discover this intelligent object which mobilizes its attention to the sequence of events in its internal processes, particularly focussing on the events at the beginning and end of its gastrointestinal tract to which he assumes all the other organs are mysteriously synchronised. But it is particularly drawn to this polarised part because it notices it can deploy its energy to influence its wayward tendencies (indigestion, pain, diarrhoea, constipation, flatulence and therefore the smell of its excreta). This latter becomes a prime indicator of the health, and by implication, the health and growth of the organs.

The metapsychology of the neonate is now in a position to employ its identification with the extraneous intelligence to initiate the process of learning from experience using these primary indicators of the smell of faeces and flatus. The rhythmic experience of the mother's discernible reaction varying from repugnance to pleasure makes an impact on the baby's experience of its polarised internal events, drawing its attention to these primary indicators of odour and nappy sensations to assume the role of experience, personal and social, combined to learn – not to be dominated by the sensations internally but to integrate them with his social experience. He will learn to resist the impulse to premature expulsion which results in wetness, irritation of the skin of the bottom and a variety of unpleasure both social and personal. He will learn to wait, not to expel but to wait for the faeces and rectum to be ready for effortless extrusion of the formed, sweet-smelling, attractively formed and pointed stool which mother will greet with delight.

This experience of mutuality is the prototype of creative triumph, its reward. What the baby learns is in effect to trust the intelligently organised physiology of its organs and to believe in the mother's judgment about suitable food more than its own sensuality. 'You don't like the taste but it is good for you.' This attitude is backed by the mother's cultural experience and is a major demotion of sensuality as a basis for judgment by the baby. The birth of trust *vs*. opinion.

CHAPTER EIGHT

Models of dependence in a family[1]

(1981)

I had recently moved Dr M's already extremely early morning session back another twenty minutes, so that he could get home in time to look after the children while his wife went to her consulting-room to see a new patient who could come at no other time. Thus a chain of accommodation had been set up from myself to Dr M to his children, to his wife, to her patient. Dr M knew my home circumstances and understood that I might oversleep, in which case I preferred that he rang the front-door bell and wait for me to appear, rather than to follow his own bent of allowing me to 'sleep on', since this had already proved to contain such a degree of patronising poor old Daddy that the analysis had stagnated for weeks thereafter. I had forgotten to mention however that the Meltzer-Harris bell was non-functional, and he should therefore ring the Harris-Williams one.

At his first session of the week he rang the Meltzer-Harris bell and I did not appear. So he returned home after some twenty

1 Written 1981; first published in *Sincerity: Collected Papers of Donald Meltzer,* ed. A. Hahn (Karnac, 1994). For models of the child in the family in the community see *The Educational Role of the Family* (Harris Meltzer Trust, 2013).

minutes and rang me towards the end of the session time 'to make sure everything was all right'. The following session he was unusually punctual and, after my apology, he asked again for reassurance that 'everything was all right' and then described the events of the previous morning. Two patterns of anxiety emerged clearly: one was that I was carrying too heavy a load of responsibility and that it might either exhaust me or affect me in some psychosomatic way. An image emerged as of the strong man in the acrobatic team at the circus on whose shoulders the other five members of the team are poised. Second was the anxiety about the children. What if he should be delayed by traffic going home? Should his wife wait for his arrival, or was it all right for her to go to her consulting-room, which was in a house just two doors away? But that did leave the children alone in the house, although probably only for a few minutes, and in all likelihood still asleep. But what if they awoke and found neither mummy nor daddy at home? Might it be a shattering experience? Even the controlled and informed circumstances of the previous session had been quite shaking to him, a sane adult. And anyhow, it was illegal to leave small children unattended.

And so it appeared that he was the second member of the acrobatic team standing on the strong man's shoulder and doing his juggling act, in danger of dropping and shattering his plates. His wife, in turn, had a second predicament. It had been somewhat difficult to find a training case in their part of North London, and she felt it was quite urgent that she finish her training, since the expenses of it were running them into debt. Anyhow, the patient seemed rather exacting and perhaps not well motivated to come five times per week. She had to balance the welfare of the children against these factors in her training, relying on her husband to keep the children safe while she balanced the Training Committee and the patient. So the other members of the acrobatic team came into view: the wife on Dr M's shoulders supporting a rigid beam called a Training, on either end of which were balanced a Training Committee and a Patient, neither of great stability in the act. I was seen as in danger of being crushed, the children of being shattered, and the patient or Training Committee of being lost for lack of motivation or investment in the success of the act.

After I had summarised his ruminations and described his three models of dependence as 'supporting', 'juggling', and 'balancing', his associations turned towards his father, full of admiration for his vitality and the breadth of his interests despite his advanced age. He had known Jung. Well, at least he had met him. Probably not an equally memorable event for Jung as for his father. Had the analyst ever known Jung? Or Freud? His father had dabbled with the I-Ching cards. He does enjoy his father's company and is puzzled that he does not arrange to spend more time with him.

I suggested that this failure to use the opportunity had something to do with denying his father's advanced age on the grounds of his vitality and retirement; that he was no longer the strong man in an acrobatic act, taking the strain. He then spoke of his mother's equal vitality and interests: CND, feminism, race relations; but without the same tone of admiration he had bestowed on his father. I commented that his mother and father did not seem to him to belong to the same acrobatic team, and he could not imagine himself ever having been able to stand on both their shoulders, since they were so far apart. That might make a far more stable situation, though of course not so spectacular for circus purposes.

The anxieties implicit in this model of dependence and of family structure are self-evident: the strong man overestimates his strength; the plate-children are too fragile; the training case and Committee are too little motivated with regard to the success of the act; and even if the burden were to be shared between the mother and father, they would have to be so close in their interests and attitudes to enable the children to span their relationship – i.e. to resolve their oedipal conflicts by virtue of lack of conflict because mummy and daddy are identical in their meaning and functions.

But is not the basic model unsatisfactory in a fundamental way? It pictures the family structure as a hierarchic one, standing on its head – as it were, an upside-down pyramid. It is a basic assumption group: dependence. You might say that its basic assumption could be stated as: the law of gravity must be overcome if the family is to present a spectacular act to the watching world. Notice also that in this model the roles and functions are rigidly determined and cannot be altered once assumed, without dismantling the entire arrangement (catastrophic change).

The purpose of this exposition shows, in a rather caricatural manner, the way in which, at a moment of crisis (in this case, a trivial one) a family group can dissolve into a basic assumption group.

CHAPTER NINE

Family patterns and modes of learning[1]

(1986)

T his chapter aims first to display the classification of family patterns we described in the 'Model of the child-in-the-family-in-the-community', and then to explore the relation of these patterns to learning processes and corresponding educational conflicts. The theoretical model employed was the Kleinian–Bionic model as described in *The Kleinian Development.* Family life was envisioned as a more or less stable organisation of three general types: (1) the family proper (couple family); (2) the narcissistic gang; (3) the basic assumption group. Within these three types of organisation we made the distinction between individuals occupying special roles and fulfilling particular functions. The roles are assumed to comprise culturally defined prerogatives, responsibilities and privileges, and therefore variable from culture to culture.

---

1   Extract from 'Family patterns and cultural educability', first published in *Studies in Extended Metapsychology* (1986), where it summarises the 'Model of the child-in-the-family-in-the-community', written in 1976, commissioned by the Organisation of Economic and Cultural Development of the United Nations. For the complete text of the Model in context see *The Educational Role of the Family: A Psychoanalytical Model* by Donald Meltzer and Martha Harris (Harris Meltzer Trust, 2013).

The functions, however, we named as follows:

(i) generating love;
(ii) promulgating hate;
(iii) promoting hope;
(iv) sowing despair;
(v) containing depressive pain;
(vi) emanating persecutory anxiety;
(vii) thinking;
(viii) creating lies and confusion.

On the basis of this three-type organisational model and eight pattern dynamic concept we were able to describe in outline the structure and functioning of the individuals in the family in the community, subdividing each disturbed organisational type into six sub-types, or thirteen sub-types in all.

The avowed intention of any family grouping is to nurture the development of its members for the preservation of the group either through harmonious integration with, destructive attacks upon, or parasitism on, the surrounding milieu, human and non-human. This nurturing must involve its members in learning, and this learning may take place inside or outside the family grouping; it may be formal or informal, noticed or unnoticed. Acquisition of knowledge and skills may contribute to development of the personality and thus to status, or it may confer *de facto* operational status, or status may be acquired by other means as if the status itself conferred skills and knowledge which do not in fact exist (hereditary status for instance). Thus roles and functions may coincide, overlap or diverge. Skills and knowledge always have both internal world and external world significance but particular aspects of skills and knowledge vary in their balance with regard to these two types of significance, or they may be confused with one another (as in the case, say, of a tribal medicine man or a present-day bank manager).

Psychoanalytical studies of the life of individuals suggest that there are a large number of ways in which alterations in the skills and knowledge may come about, some of which we can describe with some richness and precision. These various methods of organisation are probably all, from the most primitive to the most sophisticated, used to some degree by every individual of at least minimum intelligence, but psychoanalytical experience shows clearly that the character is deeply etched by the preferred modes of learning and that these preferred modes are in turn deeply influenced by the modes current in the nurturing family group and its state of organisation. We will now try to describe these modes of learning and in so doing make explicit the learning theory which is implicit in the Kleinian–Bionic model of the mind.

Modes of learning

(1) Learning from experience

Following Bion's classic description we would emphasise that learning from experience modifies the person because it is the result of an *emotional* experience in which the chaotic sense data and the persecutory anxieties pursuant to the confusion are submitted to an object, either an internal object or an external object carrying a parental transference, for sorting. The learning consequent has therefore *the meaning of an item of introjective identification* since not only is the immediate problem resolved (secondary learning of knowledge or skill) but also something is learned of the modes of thought employed in the resolution (primary learning: Wittgenstein's 'Now I can go on'). The dependent relation to the internal or external tutor requires a struggle from the paranoid-schizoid to a depressive orientation (Bion's Ps↔D) since the meaning and significance must be entertained as an aesthetic experience.

(2) Learning by projective identification

Ranged in order of increasing primitiveness the next mode of learning would be through the employment of the omnipotent phantasy of projective identification first described by Melanie Klein in 1946 ('Notes on some schizoid mechanisms'). Since the motivation for this type of learning is often envy of the object's superior capacities, and since the aim is the immediate acquisition of these skills or knowledge, the result is often a delusional overestimation of the desired acquisition. Nonetheless projective identification does enable the subject to go through the motions of the admired skill or knowledge and thus to achieve some degree of mechanical reproduction of the performance of the object's human (or animal) capability, albeit a caricature. This caricatural aspect derives from the lack of authenticity of the emotionality intrinsic to the performance and may, in the case of children, appear comic; in the hands of the comedian it becomes satire.

(3) Learning by obsessional collecting

Since the obsessional state of mind employs omnipotent means of controlling its objects in the service of evasion of oedipal conflict, it is given to sorting, cataloguing and collecting, but in so doing deprives objects of their freedom and vitality. Such lifeless collections of objects, facts and recollections have no utility in themselves but may become a source for non-obsessional utilisation having, so to speak, a secondary value. The obsessional person may be highly prized by his community for his performance of this type of donkey-work but is inevitably replaced by some mechanical contraption. It is important to stress that obsessional sorting and collecting of objects and facts can only employ an index of manifest qualities since deeper meaning and significance always require a creative conjunction scintillating with oedipal significance, and thus of anxiety, for their apprehension (i.e. the aesthetic level).

(4) Learning by submission to a persecutor

Much of the learning to which children are submitted is experienced by them in this mode, some times called the 'stick-and-carrot' method of pedagogy, more or less benevolent but structurally tyrannical. While the mechanics of the learning may be so achieved, rebelliousness and negativism are engendered so that the consequences tend to be of two sorts: either the acquisition is jettisoned from the mind as soon as the tyranny is escaped; or a projective identification with the persecutor leads to the skills and knowledge being used in an aggressive and tyrannical way. It is not certain whether the more primitive form of learning by conditioning does actually take place in human beings, as it clearly does in lower animals, since momentary and seemingly automatic (unthinking) obedience can simulate the phenomena of conditioning seen at submental (autonomic) levels.

(5) Learning by stealing and scavenging

The senses may be utilised in a secretive way for the acquisition of skills and knowledge. This produces secondarily a considerable inhibition of the utilisation of whatever is acquired since its display is felt tantamount to confession of guilt. This stealing can be modified by a phantasy of scavenging for valuable things that others foolishly throw away. Inevitably this tends to be confined to items of recherché or dubious value, the exotic or anachronistic. The sense of lack of social integration verging on tramp or pariah often accompanies activities built upon such a method of acquisition.

(6) Learning by adhesive identification

Esther Bick in her 1968 paper on skin function described a second method of narcissistic identification more primitive than projective identification and based upon very different motives. She described people whose internal objects were such poor containers and thus provided so little emotional endoskeleton to the personality that they were forced to hold their personality together by other means, one of which was through the phantasy of adhering to the surface of external objects. This seems to correspond closely to what Helene Deutsch described in her famous paper on the 'as if' personality type. This adhesive phantasy produces a type of identification with the superficial, socially visible qualities of the object but not with its mental qualities or states of mind. The behaviour that results is so immediate and so contingent on the presence or vividness of the external object as to deserve the description 'mimicry' Its manifestations in the behaviour of autistic children has been described in *Explorations in Autism*. It is suitable for the learning of social roles but cannot foster the capability for social functions.

Family functions and relationships

Our next task must be to educe some general principles governing the relationships in family groups which tend to favour the utilisation of one or other of these six modes of learning in the members of the family. We will then attempt to relate these general principles to the chief sub-types of families that have been described in the 'Model'. The course we have chosen for the elucidation of general principles is to apply our eight categories of emotional functions to the six types of learning to see if they have any discernible relationship. It would then be an almost mechanical task to apply these conjunctions of learning type and function type to the family sub-types.

(1) Generating love

Where love is generated or diffused in the social atmosphere either by an individual through his relation to internal objects or by coupled relationship, security and therefore the possibility of dependence is fostered. But the richness and generosity displayed also evoke envy. Therefore a delicate balance is set up between tendencies to introjective and projective identification in the dependent members. This balance seems to be particularly affected by the loving person's capacity to allow the dependent members to experience the mental pains of their inferiority and neediness, to allow both space and time before helpful intervention.

(2) Promulgating hate

This function, which consists in attacking the living links within the group by playing upon the feelings aroused in frustration, tends always to generate a gang, either by direct leadership or eminence grise activity. Such gangs are intrinsically tyrannical and utilise threat and seduction to bind their internal organisation. Since the destructive skills are essentially simpler than constructive ones, the learning process by submission to the leader is rapid and gratifying to dependent members of the family sub-gang.

(3) Promoting hope

 Hopefulness as an emotion, and optimism as its characterological attitude, seems to have its roots in a sense of the positive balance between constructive and destructive forces in the individual and group. It is easily disturbed by external events of a tragic nature, even more so when these are imponderable strokes of fate rather than when their human agency is clear. Therefore the maintenance of hope as a quality of family atmosphere depends upon some member being able to maintain a sense of proportion, both in the longitudinal and global sense. An atmosphere of hope fosters aspiration and willingness to risk positions of safety, to deploy vitality and resources, and thus stimulates the thirst for knowledge and skills. Its manic simulation in complacency, religiosity and denial of tragedy has an opposite effect. No quality so draws the dependent members towards introjective identification as resilient hopefulness in a parental (or even a child) figure, for it displays courage in the face of consequences, a more convincing stance than courage in the face of danger.

(4) Sowing despair

Pessimism, born of a sense of either impregnable rigidity of the system or overwhelming destructive forces, poisons the atmosphere of a family group and drives its members towards security operations. This tendency favours obsessional mechanisms of learning but also the type of leaving-the-field characteristic of scavenging. In its more extreme forms this retreat may extend to external as well as psychic reality and favour the quasi-theological clinging of the basic assumption group. The learning of irrelevant skills and the acquisition of delusional knowledge may then alienate the family and its members from the culture, with the exception of items useful for a parasitic or destructive relation to the community.

(5) Containing depressive pain

The modulation of depressive pain in a family group is characteristically a function of the parents but with surprising frequency is found to be exercised by one of the children, sometimes in a way which has the appearance of an emotional illness (as for instance after a death in the family). Since this modulation within tolerable limits is a precondition for the employment of learning from experience by dependent members, its failure tends to set in motion fragmenting forces within the group as persecutory depression circulates and irritability increases. When unity of the family declines egocentricity flourishes and engenders delinquent attitudes. Scavenging and stealing, and the modes of learning stimulated by them, replace identificatory learning processes in the 'every man for himself' atmosphere. The materialistic ambitiousness of the children in a disorganised immigrant family would exemplify this state. But where psychopathology in the mother takes the form of extreme fragility, adhesive processes are set in motion in young children and can persist even in the face of subsequent recovery or strengthening of the mother.

(6) Emanating persecutory anxiety

Any member of a family who has a sense of present terror may serve as a focus for this emotion, either by exuding the anxiety into the atmosphere or by projecting it through terrorising younger or weaker members. The sense of supra-parental forces of catastrophe so undermines both the roles and functions of the parental figure that an atmosphere of incipient panic, of apocalyptic dangers, can pervade. Whether the dangers be medical, financial, social or political, the atmosphere of helplessness paralyses learning functions of all but the most mimetic type. Adhesive identifications with figures outside the family can be seen when such situations make contact with community facilities.

(7) Thinking

While this function can be performed by anyone in the family in default by the actual parent, the capability soon runs out if the problems become complex, or when the family is in a dislocated relation to the community, or if the community itself is in disarray. A member who displays a capacity for thought quickly accrues transference significance, quite irrespective of age, and thus undertakes parental functions with or without usurping parental status. In the absence of this function the family must depend on traditional values, modes of behaviour, or seek advice outside its structure. In the face of the disintegration of traditional patterns of family life (in immigrant groups or where Church affiliation has withered), professional thinkers-about-family-matters come into great demand with as yet inadequate equipment to fulfil this task.

(8) Creating lies and confusion

Since the creating of lies and confusion seems to develop as a talent in quite young children while the capacity for thought is still sparingly existent in their elders, family organisation is constantly threatened by the liar in its midst. The detection of lies, except for factual ones, being so difficult as still to evade the skills of psychoanalysts, it is not surprising to see the havoc that lying can wreak in a family. The uncertainty it throws into the atmosphere easily metamorphoses into cynicism about the value of truth, and poisons the ethical quality of family life. This has a destructive influence on the impetus to learning since confabulation seems to be so powerful. This essentially psychopathic tendency, asocial where it is not antisocial, seems even to make a game of un-learning what has already been acquired and perhaps corresponds to what Bion has called 'alpha-function in reverse'.

Any one of these eight functions may be implemented by actions or communications, open or covert; by truth or lies (that is by actions or statements whose meaning is known to be false). At any one moment any of these eight functions tends to be delegated to individual members, bringing them into functional conflict with their opposite number. Where individuals are at the moment attaching themselves to someone else to perform a function for them we will speak of functional dependence. Functions may be assumed by the individual or may be imposed upon him by other members. Functions may be in abeyance, being carried out by no one, thus forming a focus of chaos with implicit catastrophic anxiety. We may now turn our attention to the description of the family proper (the Couple Family) and some of its various types of imitations, caricatures, distortions and perversions.

The couple family

At the moment when the family is presided over by a couple (not necessarily the actual parents) this combination will be seen to carry between them the functions of generating love, promoting hope, containing depressive pain, and thinking. The capacity of the couple to perform these functions will be felt to require their periodic withdrawal into privacy, supposed to be sexual and mysterious. The times when they are obliged to be apart produces a hovering sword-of-Damocles atmosphere while their conjunction arouses a constant expectation of 'new baby' members of the family. The history of their courtship is of mythological interest to the dependent members, giving form to their hopes of the future.

The four introjective *functions* of the couple – generating love, promoting hope, containing pain, and thinking – are not felt to subdivide into masculine and feminine aspects but rather to be arranged in a more linear way, with the maternal person taking the brunt of the children's projections and the father being the end of the line for these mental waste products (Harry Truman's 'the buck stops here').

All the catastrophic anxiety of the dependent members tends to centre on the mother, regardless of the intensity of love that may be felt for the father and the depressive anxieties that may accompany it. Therefore any evidence of debility in the mother tends to be blamed on the father's possible or suspected inadequacies. On the other hand debility in the father is taken as evidence that the system is being overloaded with hate and projected persecution and encourages polarisation among the dependent members, with a scapegoating tendency.

The growth of all members of the family, as evidenced by carefully monitored and frequently discussed indicators of physical, social, intellectual and emotional development, is necessary to maintain the sense of security which is intrinsic to the family and is felt to be utterly independent of the community despite the overall optimistic and benevolent view taken of the natural and social milieu. Thus the family is felt to be mobile potentially, even though it may be tenderly attached to the home or landscape or community of friends and neighbours. If opportunity glows on the horizon a pioneer atmosphere begins to scintillate, akin in feeling to the times when the mother is pregnant.

The overall relation to the community is felt to proceed through the individual members moving about – at school or at work or shopping, etc. – as representatives of the family. Their individual identities (given name) are secondary in significance to their family identity (surname), not as an indicator of status but as a burden of responsibility. It is not so much a matter of 'what will the neighbours think?', as of 'letting the side down', in the business of contributing to the general ethos of the community.

The great vulnerability of the couple resides in the unique identity of each individual – for the death of a child seems to be the one unbearable stress (Wordsworth's 'We are seven'). Even a miscarriage or a stillbirth can have a shattering effect upon the joyousness and commence a deterioration in ethos, relationships, cohesiveness, from which recovery may seem impossible. It has a more devastating effect than, say, the impact of a defective child, the development of a schizophrenic illness in a child, or the delinquency or defection of a member.

The relation of learning types to family patterns

For simplicity we here draw up a list of these correlations:[2]

The Couple Family	Introjective identification
The Dolls' House Family	Introjective identification
The Matriarchal Family	Projective identification and submission to persecutors
The Patriarchal Family	Submission to persecutors and scavenging
The Gang Family	Stealing and adhesive identification
The Reversed Family	Stealing and scavenging; also projective identification
Basic Assumption Families	Projective and adhesive identification

It must be stressed that this attempt at classification is part of model-making, based on clinical and life experience, intended for use as a guide for framing and evaluating research studies. One such study we have ourselves proposed. While it is all impressionistic it has the advantage of catching the problem in a

2 These types or levels of family organisation are described in detail in *The Educational Role of the Family* (2013).

cross-fire of multiple vertices or points of view. It also has the virtue of being highly dynamic, seeking only to afford a method of describing the momentary or cross-sectional state of individuals in the family in the community, recognising that these are highly unstable and at best can be taken as trends. It is also clear, therefore, that this system of classification, largely based as it is on the model of the mind derived from the extended metapsychology of the Freud–Klein–Bion development in psychoanalysis, is in no way exclusive of other systems drawn from sociology or anthropology. Rather it would be hoped that it would lend itself easily to combination with other approaches. Certainly it does not begin to be exhaustive, the variations in family patterns from these basic ones being as numerous as the flowers of the field.

The first thing of interest that can be said with confidence is that the order of classification given above corresponds precisely with the developmental fertility of the family milieu with respect to the growth of individuals comprising it, grown-ups and children alike. And in this sense the patterns are self-perpetuating with respect to cultural achievement of the individual children as the parents of the next generation. The exception to this dictum resides in the degree to which rebellion against the family pattern is stimulated in the children. It would seem to be greatest in the patriarchal family, somewhat less in the matriarchal, dormant in the doll's house family, and virtually absent, because turned against the community, in the gang, reversed, and basic assumption families.

It is also of interest to note that the degree of harmonious relation to the benevolent aspects of the community diminishes as one goes down the list and reverses within the patriarchal group. This also means that the children of these families will tend to be mobile upward or downward in their attitudes to skills, knowledge, economic and social status compared with their parents, in accord with this degree of harmony or conflict with the community, its resources and demands.

Similarly the type of psychiatric disturbance to be expected in the children of the family would slide from the neurotic symptomatology of the doll's house children, through the character disorders of the matriarch–patriarch group becoming delinquent (gang family), perverted (reversed family), and borderline or psychopathic in the basic assumption families. These correlations have become more apparent in recent years in psychoanalytical work as we have been able to consider the patient's organisation, internal and external, with respect to groups. This extension of our awareness of phenomena has diminished the tendency to see the psychopathology of the child in a one-to-one relation to that of the parents (cf. the concept of the schizophrenogenic mother no longer seems useful).

In a sense the epidemiological significance of the classification depends not only on the self-perpetuating aspect of each of the family pattern types (in fact this quality is, gratefully, strongest of all in the couple family) but on the variable of the capacity of the family grouping to allow the individual child to enter into transference relations with other figures, present ones like teachers and therapists, or absent ones like cultural or historic heroes outside the family unit or extended family. This factor is the nemesis of the child guidance approach and lies behind the urgency with which a wide spectrum of therapeutic techniques and a precise method of assessment for their deployment is being sought.

Finally it is hoped that this model may serve to give form to studies of our educational system which may make it possible to get beyond the conflicts arising from philosophic and ideological bias in revising methods of pedagogy. When filled out with clinical evidence to correct and refine its crude impressionistic quality, such a model of the individual child in his family within the community could serve to frame a system at once flexible, workable and geared to the changing needs of the community as well as to the development of the individual.

CHAPTER TEN

Identification and socialisation in adolescence[1]

(1967)

S urely, it will be said – and rightly – the analytic consulting-room, in its heat of infantile intimacy, is not the place
to study the social behaviour of adolescents. But it can,
through clarification of the internal processes – of motivation
and expectation, identification and alienation – throw a special
and unparalleled light upon social processes to aid the sociolo-
gist, educator, psychiatrist, and all those persons of the adult
community whose task it is to preserve the boundaries of the
adolescent world and foster the growth and development of
those still held within its vortex.

Our times reveal more clearly than other historical periods the
truth of the existence of an 'adolescent world' as a social structure, the inhabitants of which are the happy-unhappy multitude
caught betwixt the 'unsettling' of their latency period and the
'settling' into adult life, the perimeter of which may not unrea-
sonably be defined, from the descriptive point of view, as the
establishment of mating and child rearing. From the metapsychological point of view of psychoanalysis, stripped as it is of

---

[1] First published in *Contemporary Psychoanalysis,* 3: 96–103 (1967); reprinted
in *Sexual States of Mind* (1973).

social and moral evaluation, this passage from latency to adulthood may be described most forcefully in structural terms, whose social implications this chapter is intended to suggest.

The developmental pathways which traverse this world of adolescence lead from splitting in the self to integration, in relation to objects which, also by integration, are transformed from a multitude of part-objects to a family of whole objects in the internal world. Upon this model the external relationships must be regulated. As long as splitting of self and objects is still considerable, the experience of self will be highly fluctuating, depending on the dominance of one or other of the three types of psychic experience of identity in consciousness (described below). In a sense one may say that the centre of gravity of the experience of identity shifts – and in the adolescent it shifts wildly and continually.

This phenomenon, the continual shifting of the centre of gravity of the sense of identity, produces the characteristic quality of emotional instability seen in adolescence and since it is based on the underlying splitting processes, the varying states of mind are in very little contact with one another. Hence the adolescent's gross incapacity to fulfil commitments to others, to carry through resolutions of his own or to comprehend why he cannot be entrusted with responsibilities of an adult nature. He cannot fully experience that the person who did not fulfil and the person who undertook to fulfil the commitment were the same person, namely himself. He therefore feels a continual grievance of the 'brother's keeper' type.

His solution to this terrible state is a flight into group life where the various parts of himself can be externalised into the various members of the 'gang'. His own role becomes simplified greatly, though not completely, for status and function in the group is in flux to a certain extent. This flight-to-the-group phenomenon is equally evident dynamically in the adolescent who is not apparently a member of any gang, for, by being the 'pariah', he fulfils a role which the gang formation requires: that of the totally alienated psychotic part of the personality in relation to those who are integrated in the gang. The isolate in turn projects his own more healthy parts.

I would remind you that this is not a descriptive definition of an age group but a metapsychological description of personality organisation typical of this age group; for we may meet 'latency' in a fifty-year-old and 'adolescence' at nine, structurally. The most important fact to be kept in mind in the following discussion is the transition from excessive and rigid splitting in latency, through the fluidity of adolescence in that matrix of personality where the more orderly and resilient splitting and differentiation of adult personality organisation must eventually be fashioned in order for the sense of identity to be established without rigidity.

The experience of identity is complex in structure and various in quality. Its unconscious basis we express by the concept of 'identification' on the one hand, and the experience of 'self' on the other. It contains both characterological and body-image facets and must be taken, in toto, as a summation of momentary states of mind, an abstraction of highly variable integration – from individual to individual, from moment to moment. The experience of identity also cannot exist in isolation, but only as foreground to the world of objects, internal and external – and to the laws of psychic and external reality.

There are three types of experiences which carry the feeling of identity: the experience of a part of the self; of identification with an object by introjection; and of identification with an object by projection. Each of the three has a very distinctive quality. The experience of a part of the self carries a feeling of limitation akin to littleness, tinged with loneliness. Introjective identification contains an aspirational element, tinged with anxiety and self-doubt. But the state of mind achieved by projective identification is fairly delusional in its quality of completeness and uniqueness. The attendant anxieties, largely claustrophobic and persecutory, are held very separately in the mind from the identity experience.

I wish to come back now to the more central problem: the underlying severe confusion at all levels with which the adolescent is contending. As I have said, with the breakdown of the obsessional, rigid, and exaggerated splitting characteristic of latency structure, an uncertainty characteristic of the pre-oedipal development reappears with regard to the differentiations internal-external, adult-infantile, good-bad, and male-female. In addition, perverse tendencies due to confusion of erogenous zones, compounded with confusion between sexual love and sadism, take the field. This is all 'in order', as it were: the group life presents a modulating environment vis-à-vis the adult world and distinct from the child-world, well-equipped to bring this seething flux gradually into a more crystallised state—if the more psychotic type of confusion of identity due to massive projective identification does not play too great a role. To illustrate this I will shortly describe two cases briefly.

But first to clarify the concept. Where the reappearance of masturbation brings with it a strong tendency, driven by infantile oral envy, to abandon the self and seise an object's identity by intrusion into it, the stage is set for a type of confusional anxiety which all adolescents experience to some extent. This confusion centres on their bodies and appears with the first pubic hair, the first breast growth, first ejaculation, and so forth. Whose body is it? In other words, they cannot distinguish with certainty their adolescent state from infantile delusions-of-adulthood induced by masturbation with attendant projective identification into internal objects. This is what lies behind the adolescent's slavish concern about clothes, make-up and hair-style, hardly less in the boys than in the girls.

Where this mechanism is very strongly operative and especially where it is socially 'successful', the building up of the 'false self' of which Winnicott has spoken takes place.

Case material

Rodney entered analysis at eighteen after the complete academic failure of his first year at university. He was, two years later, able to regain a place and continue his education; but in the analysis scholastic failure had promptly appeared as the least of his difficulties. His latency period had been built on a severe split in his family adjustment, as he had been a devoted, endlessly helpful and unfailingly polite son among the otherwise rather stormy children. In fact in his own eyes, he was never a child but a father-surrogate in all matters other than sexuality. To compensate, he appropriated as his due an absolute privacy and self-containment which, with the onset of puberty, became converted into a cover of absolute secrecy for a florid delinquent bisexual life, while his family behaviour remained unchanged – now he was a 'manly chap' instead of a 'manly little chap'.

In dividing himself among his gang he retained as his 'self' the worst, most envious and cynical bit of himself. Consequently his relation to others tended to be both forceful and corrupting. The best parts of himself tended to remain projected into younger siblings, from whom he maintained a severe, protective distance.

More delusional states of identity occurred relatively infrequently and only under special circumstances – if he were driving his mother's car, or entertaining friends in an outbuilding he had been given as a study. These states could be dangerous indeed, physically and morally, but were soon recognised in the analysis and could be avoided. The establishment of contact with good parts in a therapeutic alliance with the analyst and with internal objects could take place. Progress was steady and rewarding.

Paul, on the other hand, had entered analysis in pre-puberty owing to severe character restriction, with obsessional symptoms, nocturnal rituals, obvious effeminacy – all of which had existed for years but had been worsened by the break-up of the parents' marriage. The first period of analysis with another analyst utilising play technique had been virtually non-verbal. In those sessions he had been preoccupied with painting and art, producing a few pictures analysable in content but mainly endless preparations-for-painting consisting of mixing colours, making colour charts—in fact, concretely being daddy's artist-penis preparing the semen for the coming intercourse. As his symptoms had lessened and his school adjustment and work had improved he broke off the analysis, returning to it only three years later, when after passing his O-levels and working his way to being vice-captain of his school, he found himself confronted with A-levels for which he was totally unprepared.

What had happened in the intervening time was that the building up of the school-self of athlete-artist-vice-captain had become totally time-consuming. It had to be compensated for by a gradual retrenchment from all academic subjects requiring thought or exact knowledge, in favour of those which he felt just required talent or were based on vague statistics. He had become unable to study and his time at home and in school was consumed in the business of preparation or the postures of absorption. His paranoia, particularly in relation to laughter, had to be hidden and his own mocking laugh – irreproachably tolerant in timbre – kept a steady stream of projection of feelings of humiliation penetrating into others.

Analytic work to gather together his infantile parts into the transference and to differentiate the delusions-of-adulthood from his true adult personality was the most tedious uphill work. Every separation brought a renewed flight by projective identification: represented in dreams by intruding into gardens, climbing into houses, leaving the main road for a trackless swamp, and so forth. For instance, in a Thursday evening session he had experienced a reawakening of gratitude toward his mother for providing the analysis, along with guilt about the motor scooter he had insisted on having and the hours of analysis he had missed or wasted. It had been his unusually strong reaction to the analysis of a dream which showed clearly that the preponderance of his infantile parts wanted analysis, not masturbation. In the dream *the crowd at a school dance was sitting at tables demanding food rather than going into the ballroom to 'twist'*. By Friday, however, he had whipped himself into a state of arrogant contempt for the analysis because the analyst did not realise that Paul had now finally emerged from the chrysalis of 'student'. His art teacher by contrast had said that his new picture was the first to show a style of his own rather than mimicry of others' styles. Relentlessly then, he would spend the weekend mixing paints.

Paul presented a façade of social integration – the school captain – while Rodney seemed delinquent, corrupted, and isolated from society. But in fact, closer scrutiny shows that Rodney had a gang in which his identity was disseminated and from which it could be retrieved; while Paul had only 'friends' who were his enforced colleagues while he was vice-captain and later captain of the school. In fact he was isolated – 'well-liked', to use the immortal phrase of Willy Lomas in Arthur Miller's *Death of a Salesman*.

These two cases are intended to show the important role of the group as a social pattern in adolescence, indicating that no matter how delinquent or anti-social it may appear vis-à-vis the adult world, it is a holding position in relation to the splitting processes. By means of the dissemination of parts of the self into members of the group, amelioration of the masturbatory urge is achieved and social processes are set in train which foster the gradual lessening of the splitting, diminution of the omnipotence, and easing of persecutory anxiety through achievement in the real world.

We must however turn back to our analytic experience at the other pole of the adolescent process to comprehend the basis of this dissemination. Experience in carrying latency children into puberty during analysis reveals this in a brilliant way which I will describe by means of a third case:

Juliet had come to analysis at the age of seven for deeply schizoid character difficulties which rendered her doll-like in appearance and demeanour, utterly submissive to excellent but highly idealised parents. This façade was fissured in two areas: explosion of faecal smearing on rare occasions, and a witch-like hegemony over a younger sister and her little friends.

Six years of the most arduous analytic work broke through this, enabling her true femininity, artistic talents, and rich imagination to emerge by the time of her menarche. But her masculinity formed the basis of her social adaptation to peers, as shown by the formation of a gang of five girls, all intelligent, attractive, and athletic, who became the 'trouble-makers' of her girls' school. The general pattern of a very revealing dream of that time was subsequently repeated, again and again. She seemed in the dream to be *one of five convict men who were confined in a flimsy structure made of slats at the top of a tall tree. But every night they escaped and prowled about the village, returning unbeknown to their captors before dawn.*

This dream could be related to earlier material regarding masturbatory habits in which her fingers, in bed at night, explored the surfaces and orifices of her body, often accompanied by conscious adventuresome phantasies.

Two years later, when her femininity had established itself in the social sphere as well, she attended her first unchaperoned party, where the boys were somewhat older; drinking occurred, and sexual behaviour became rather open. To her surprise she behaved with a coolness and provocativeness which earned her the shouted epithet of 'frigid tart' from a boy whose attempt to feel under her skirt she had skilfully repulsed.

That night she dreamed that *five convicts were confined to a wooden shed from which they were released by a bad squire on condition that they would steal fruit from the women with fruit stalls in the village and bring the loot to him.*

Here one can see that the delinquent organisation of the masculine masturbating fingers had been projected into the boys of the party by her 'frigid tart' behaviour. The fact that the phantasies acted out were infantile and pregenital (anal and oral) was clearly indicated by the stealing of food, from the bottom, a theme well known from the earlier years of analytic work.

The masturbatory theme, the personification of the fingers, seems in fact to turn up with extraordinary frequency in our analytic work and would lead us to the expectation that the typical 'gang' of the adolescent would tend, by unconscious preference, to contain five members, or multiples of this number. In other terminology we might say that the gestalt of the adolescent gang would tend most strongly to 'close' at five members.

This brief account presents some of the knowledge gained by recent analytic experience with children carried into puberty and with adolescents carried into adult life. The work was conducted within the framework of theory and technique which is an extension of the developments in psychoanalysis associated with the name of Melanie Klein. It draws very heavily on her delineation of the pregenital Oedipus conflicts, the role of splitting processes in development, and the phenomenology of projective identification as a dynamic mechanism, and may not be readily comprehended without a general understanding of her work. A most lucid description of this will be found in Hanna Segal's book [*Introduction to the Work of Melanie Klein*, 1964].

I have discussed how the return of severe splitting processes, characteristic of infancy and early childhood, which attends the adolescent flux, requires externalisation in group life so that the omnipotence and confusional states precipitated by the return of masturbation at puberty may be worked through. The implications for sociological comprehension of the 'adolescent world' as a social institution are apparent:

(1) Individual psychotherapeutic work should be directed toward the isolated individual, to promote the socialisation of his conflicts.

(2) The 'gang' formation of adolescents needs to be contained in its anti-social aspects but not to be intruded upon by adult guidance.

(3) The emergence of individuals from adolescence into adult life is facilitated by measures which lessen the conflict between the sexual aspirations toward mating and other areas of ambition.

CHAPTER ELEVEN

Note on a transient inhibition of chewing[1]

(1959)

This brief clinical paper sets out to demonstrate a critical week in the third year of analysis of a borderline schizoid case. The material represents the culmination of a certain lines of work during the previous year aimed at demonstrating psychic reality to the patient but also stands as the beginning of a period of six months characterised by marked clinical improvement outside the analysis and the most dogged resistance to any further advance within the consulting-room.

This 23-year-old single man had been continuously under psychotherapeutic care since the age of thirteen, following a breakdown at boarding school characterised by insomnia, paranoid attitudes towards other students, ruminative concern and periodic panics about his mother's safety, and complete inability to do his studies. His developmental history, though still only partly known to me, was markedly schizoid from early on, shown by such items as indifference to parents following a two-week separation at the age of three, withdrawal into intense megalomanic identifications, fear and dislike of other children,

---

1 Read to the British Psychoanalytical Society in 1959; first published in *Sincerity: Collected Papers of Donald Meltzer,* ed. A. Hahn (Karnac, 1994).

compulsive masturbation, and eating difficulties. At the time of starting the analysis, he presented a very flaccid demeanour, leptosomic body configuration, stereotypy in speech and gesture, and extreme secretiveness about his way of life and about his reasons for seeking analysis. it has been gradually revealed that he has had no sexual contacts, he views his body as horribly deformed, and practises both anal and genital masturbation along with a sadomasochistic perversion in relation to his own body and occasionally with animals. Although his somatic delusions, still incompletely known to me, seem to centre around the feeling that his body parts are repulsive and dare not be shown to others, impaired functioning also plays a role, as it also does in his complaints about his inability to make constructive use of his excellent mind. But what I wish to stress is the intactness of his ego and his body image, albeit deformed and useless. His parents are alive and well, and he makes his home with them still, as do an older sister and a younger brother.

The first eighteen months of the analysis, much to the patient's surprise, produced significant improvement in his ability to work and a lessening of the compulsion to masturbate or practise sadomasochistic perversions. To his horror he found himself coming across evidence in dreams and in the occasional hallucination of a connection between his relation to the analyst and early positive feelings towards the mother and her breast. He promptly acted-out at his new job, was sacked, and entered upon a period of rather psychotic dilapidation and semi-vagrancy for the next four months. As the analysis brought him out of this, through work on his dreams and acting-out, I was able to show him the fundamentals of psychic reality – the relation of his ego-state and body image to that of his internal objects, the connection between his instinctual life and the state of preservation of his internal object, and the connection between his relationships to internal and external objects. During this last period he twice had nocturnal psychotic experiences which, he hinted, were linked with events of his breakdown at the age of thirteen and with recurrent dreams from earlier on. On one occasion he lay awake all night fully clothed and armed with a knife for fear his parent would enter his bedroom and murder him. On a second occasion he hallucinated his mother, eyes blazing, holding a knife to his belly. During this period, as the positive maternal transference pressed into consciousness again and again, a typical configuration in his acting-out appeared: the moment positive feelings were aroused toward the analyst, they would be split off into an external person, generally at home or at work. The patient would then provoke this person into disappointing or hurting him, resulting in spoiling his internal and subsequently his external relationship to the analyst. These two nocturnal experiences mentioned were the sequellae of such acting-out with the parents.

This, in outline, is the background of the events revealed and analysed during the three days – Tuesday, Wednesday, and Thursday – to be reported. Before going into detail I shall describe the main sequence.

On the Thursday, the patient reported that he had eaten no solid food since the evening meal following the Tuesday session. That session had been devoted largely to the analysis of a dream – the 'First Lady' dream – which followed a bit of acting-out on his motorbike. The Wednesday session was given over to intense resistance growing out of a hallucinatory experience of the previous evening. This resistance also involved the withholding of a dream that followed the hallucination – the 'Delicious Jaw' dream – which emerged on the Thursday. Thus: Monday – positive feelings and acting-out; Tuesday – analysis of the 'First Lady' dream, ate dinner, hallucinatory experience in bed, dreamed of the 'Delicious Jaw' but withheld the dream from analysis on the Wednesday and was unable to eat solid foods until after it was analysed on the Thursday.

These three sessions represent the convergence of several threads of analytic work aimed at demonstrating to the patient that the defects in his body image and related impairment in mental and somatic functioning were the result of identification with mutilated internal objects, and that this identification was a defence against internal persecution which, in turn, was the result of a strong tendency to regress to part-object relationships as a defence against overwhelming depressive anxiety composed of grief, guilt and despair.

Thus we will try to demonstrate in the following material that the analysis of the 'First Lady' dream, by partially restoring the internal object as a whole object, enabled the patient to diminish his identification with it and to experience some of the despair and grief of the depressive position in the internal object relationship – the *hallucinatory experience.* The recognition that this improved relationship to his internal object had been brought about by the analyst (external object) resulted in the greedy yearning to complete the restoration by stealing from the analyst ('Delicious Jaw' dream). But this dream implied very clearly that the origin of the mutilation of his good internal object lay in his own greedy stealing introjection. This so threatened to confront him with the *guilt* of the depressive situation that identification with the mutilated object was invoked again, resulting in the inhibition to chewing solid food and associated resistance in the analytic situation.

With this route map in hand, we may now proceed with the details of the clinical material. The analysis of the Monday hour brought the patient into an unusually strong contact with feelings of admiration and envy for the fertility of the analyst's mind and the richness of the analytic process. Immediately on leaving the session, acting-out took place in which he went quite far out of his way on his motorbike to pass by the house of his previous therapist, who appears in the manifest content of the 'First Lady' dream that night. The great urgency to destroy these positive feelings through immediate acting-out was a function of the unusual intensity of the admiration.

Tuesday session

The patient reported riding past the house of his previous therapist, and associations included an incident in which he felt she had once 'sniggered' at his jokingly calling a small church a cathedral. He dreamed that night that *she had come to visit him at his home, but it was like the present consulting rom. Her husband was with her, but the patient was no sure if he entered. The patient did not notice her deformities until he put his arm around her shoulder, then noticed that her back was hunched, one foot was huge and mutilated, and she was blind. He was horrified and recalled that he had just seen a press clipping in which she was referred to as the 'First lady of the land' and wondered if it was an obituary. He was then with his father and siblings, being taught the art of killing in self-defence. The patient was crying about his therapist, but his father said to 'stop snivelling', whereupon he began a tirade against the father's callousness.*

His association to the dream was only that he felt depressed last night after his father had *failed* to laugh at a joke he had made. The session, including another dream, centred around the analysis of the depressive feelings connected with differentiating between internal and external objects and confrontation with the contrast between the 'First lady of the land' analytic mother outside, and the horrifying object he gets inside himself as a result of splitting and projecting the 'sniggering' envious part of himself into her. I also showed him how he projected the guilt into the analyst father, who is held responsible for preventing rather than fostering reparation of the mother. The detailed linking of this with the transference, the acting-out, and the content of the previous session, brought a tirade of self-pity and accusations against the analyst of callousness towards *his* suffering. This outburst of 'snivelling' through identification with the mutilated internal object did not seem to be significantly lessened by interpretation at the time. So up to this point, the patient had split off his positive maternal transference onto the previous therapist (a woman), degraded her by projecting the 'snivelling envious part of himself into her as shown by his association about the church he called a cathedral. Thus she became, internally, a hideous object, while the guilt for this attack was laid at the feet of the analyst, now in the role of father who strengthens not his capacity for love but for 'self-defence' – that is, defending the intactness of his ego against the guilt connected with his envy of the good mother. This left him 'snivelling', or in other words, filled with self-pity.

Wednesday session

This hour was given over to intense resistance, composed of overt hostility unusual for this patient. There was at first a barrage of belittling attacks on the analyst, ridiculing the previous session and the theories of psychoanalysis, denying the existence of psychic reality, asserting the accuracy of his perceptual apparatus ('even babies can see'), and defending the rational nature of all anxiety ('babies are not afraid of cats unless they have previously had bad experience with cats'). Buried in this avalanche of words was a brief mention that he'd had a 'vision' of his mother looking old and tired, her face lined and eyes hollow, looking at him without hatred but clearly unable to give him the comfort for which he was yearning. A terrible dread came over him. There was a strong opposition to acknowledging the vision as a hallucination. The interpretation of it in the transference linking it with the 'First Lady' dream and the fear of the analysis dying slowly – as he felt with his previous therapy – brought a renewed and prolonged tirade of abuse and ridicule. He was 'tired of having to correct [the analyst's] mistakes; he 'could do the analysis better by himself'; the analyst was seeking to destroy his self-confidence and independence. We can see that the transference had shifted back to the maternal, but the external analyst-mother was now experienced as being just as disappointing as the lined-cheeked, hollow-eyed internal mother – not a source of nourishment, but useful only as an object for projection of bad feelings and impulses.

Thursday session

This is the main body of the paper and will be presented in some detail. Although the interpretations are in many ways incomplete and inadequate, the patient showed unusual responsiveness to them. This can be taken as good testimony that the integrative capacities of his ego were joining in the analysis to a degree extraordinary for him.

The patient was on time, assumed his usual motionless position on the couch, and immediately reported that he had not taken any solid food since the Tuesday session. However, it was deliberate abstinence based on scientific theories concerning his body, though the analyst would probably not agree: he was too heavy, which placed a strain on his body; since it took more work to digest solid food than liquids because of the chewing and grinding inside, he was giving his digestive organs a rest through a liquid diet, and it was quite good fun.

Interpretation: The patient was claiming he was deliberately controlling his greed towards the analyst out of concern over the very rapid increase in his mental abilities, which he felt to have been the result of causing the analyst to work too hard inside

him, digesting the material that he supplied. By this he was denying what had happened, which the analyst had repeatedly shown
him was the reverse – that in his digesting of the analytic food,
he mutilated it until the sound and meaning became separated,
so that he was taking in the form without the substance, out
of envy towards the object that fed him. He felt hopeless about
being able to take inside a real mother with her breasts, but only
the milk alone from a bottle devoid of human relationship. By
splitting off this incapacity to feed properly into the realm of
actual food, he was able to deny both the seriousness of it – since
he can get adequate nourishment from liquids – and the fact
that his incapacity was also the result of an identification with an
internal object (inside) whose capacity to digest difficult material
had been in some way impaired (namely the analyst). Therefore
he could only use the analyst on the previous day as a receptacle
for his own horror about the dream and hopelessness connected
with the vision, not as a source of good analytic food.

Patient: Does not think yesterday was a waste of time. He had
a dream on Tuesday night, but the post-mortem on the 'First
Lady' dream had been much more pressing in his opinion.

Interpretation: He had felt yesterday that he was pushing
into me the responsibility for the mutilation of the First Lady
and forcing me to further dismember her, until her identity
was unrecognisable and could be fed back to him as a formless
substance.

Patient: That's not what a post-mortem is for: it is to deter-
mine the cause of death. Anyhow, in the dream, *a gaunt, middle-
aged man, a pleasant chap really, was holding another man down
while someone – perhaps himself – was removing the man's jaw
very carefully and painlessly; it seemed to be attached by a sling-like
arrangement, like two strips of bacon rind. The man offered no resistance – perhaps he was dead. Then the patient ate the jaw – probably
cooking it first; it was absolutely delicious* [with genuine feeling].
Perhaps it satisfied him so that he had had no need for solid food
since.

Interpretation: Here we could see the answer to his defence
in the Wednesday hour that in the analysis of the 'First Lady'
dream the cause of mutilation had not been revealed. The bacon
rind linked this dream to previous ones of 'Masturbating-pig'

and 'Coitus', in both of which he had felt a horror of what was being done, regarding both spoiling and greed. Much of the clinical improvement prior to the summer holiday had stemmed from a detailed analysis of his compulsive anal and genital masturbation and its effect on his relation to internal objects. These advances had been epitomised in the analysis of these two dreams eight months apart. The first was of *a 'rosy little pig' masturbating on some fresh pork, while in the background a cow was being milked by a machine.* In the second dream, *an unrecognised couple were embracing in the nude, and the patient was both masturbating between the woman's buttocks and grasping her breast with the other hand.*

Patient: Oh, there was no horror in this dream – it was pain-less; not gentlemanly perhaps, but done with consideration.

Interpretation: In order to protect against the longing and hunger for the analyst-mother outside, he had stolen his jaw to eat it at leisure, to get the meat of the analysis in order to complete by himself the restoration of his internal mother. By that act he got inside himself again another mutilated object – a jawless analyst, like a nipple-less mother, with which (if he cannot bear to look at the object to recognise who had caused the damage and perhaps to repair it) he must become identified: jawless, and unable to use his own jaw in a constructive way, as in the previous day's session and in his inability to chew solids.

(In this interpretation, in comparing the jaw of the analyst to the nipple of the mother, a reference to symbol formation was not meant. The patient knew from previous material how concretely the analyst's jaw was taken as a part-object containing the analysis. This had been most clearly seen in a dream follow-ing a session in which anxiety had been aroused, of *Frank Sinatra opening his mouth extremely wide and shouting very loud.* The patient had admired, in the dream, Sinatra's ability to dislocate his jaw, as a snake does in swallowing its victim.)

Patient: Oh, that's quite neat. A very possible interpretation, but it does not take into account all the facts – he was terrified of that vision of his mother, and he hated her for disappointing him.

Interpretation: That was a distortion of what he had reported yesterday that the vision, unlike the blazing-eyed one reported earlier, knife to belly, had not been of a frightening object but only inspired a dread that comfort would never come. His hopelessness was derived from the conviction that he could never keep that internal mother from being harmed by the envious part of himself, from his own cruelty. He was closer to acknowledging that it was the injuries to *her* inside that condemned him to a mutilated body and defective mind, regardless of the 'First Lady' goodness of what the analyst-mother could offer him outside.

This precipitated attacks of ridicule and contempt for the analyst and psychoanalysis and a re-assertion that the patient's difficulties were all due to fear, not cruelty. The only way to stop being afraid of someone was to be exactly like them, to yield to everything. In the past few weeks he had begun to free himself from this, to feel better, to be better – so of course the fear had returned, and he could not bear it any longer.

But he was forgetting that his ability to free himself from his identification with this mutilated persecutor was the result of the analysis having first rehabilitated her from the blazing-eyed mother with a knife at his belly of two years ago, to the 'neurotic invalid' of two months ago, and then to the hollow-eyed mother of two days ago. (Two months previously, there had appeared the first evidence of acknowledgement of the relation between the analyst's efforts, the improved state of his internal objects, and his own clinical improvement, along with feelings of admiration for the analytic process and the analyst's manner of carrying it out. This had all come together with greatest clarity in a dream in which the patient *was concerned with trying to extinguish a smouldering fire under the floor in his room, but without success, using a hose borrowed from his father. In the meantime the analyst had entered the room and was leading to safety a 'neurotic old invalid' woman whom the patient had not noticed before. He admired the analyst's calm and business-like manner and thought he meant to rehabilitate the woman.* What had occurred was a *renewed* mutilation: a consequence of yielding to a cruel greed in an attempt to protect himself from being hungry when alone and jealous in isolation.)

In the Friday session he was depressed, but this was quickly split off from the weekend separation onto the departure of a girl from his office. A hastily improvised and frantic sequence of sallies against the analyst, aimed at destroying all positive feeling prior to the weekend, dissolved fairly easily in the face of interpretation. The weekend was characterised by intense hunger, jealousy of siblings, and anxiety dreams showing his improved capacity to respect and protect the good food. In one dream, he *rode out into the desert on his motorbike to round up some dirty little Arab boys who had put dirt on some eggs. he made them clean up the mess. Rain immediately began to fall in the desert, and he ran out to enjoy it in the nude.*

It is of special interest to note that the motorbike used for splitting on Monday in his ride past the previous therapist's house is now used for diminishing splitting and taking responsibility for the envious 'dirty little Arab boys' part of himself.

Discussion

In the foregoing material I have presented a week of analytic work in the third year of the analysis of a severely schizoid young man – a week that shows him on the threshold of the depressive position, in contact for the first time with psychic reality and its implications, and experiencing for the first time in his analysis strong admiration and real hopefulness. But I wish to draw attention to the great danger that he is also confronting at this time: the danger of fragmentation of his ego and his objects, as against previous mutilation: that is, the danger of psychosis as opposed to character disorder, as the reconstruction of his good object brings in its wake a surge towards integration in his ego, linked to greed.

Melanie Klein writes in her paper 'On the development of mental functioning':

> Among the hated and threatening objects which the early ego tries to ward off, are those which are felt to have been injured or killed and which thereby turn into dangerous persecutors. With the strengthening of the ego and its growing capacity for integration and synthesis, the stage of the depressive position is reached. At this stage the injured object is no longer predominantly felt as a persecutor but as a loved object toward whom feelings of guilt and the urge to make reparation are experienced. (Klein, 1958, p. 241)

In this material we witness the patient's encounter with the problem of introjecting his good object, first of all spoiled by immediate destructive envious projective identification and jealous *isolation* of it (the 'First Lady' dream). Although it was not possible to demonstrate it to the patient at the time other than through the sniggering-snivelling material, subsequent material has shown clearly that the deformities-enlargements were the consequence of violent penetration into the object by the envious part of himself. The analysis of this dream corrected to some extent the damage done by projective identification but left the patient with an object only partially restored (the hallucination of the mother). The consequence was a greedy yearning to steal a part of the analyst to complete this restoration (the 'Delicious Jaw' dream).

In *Envy and Gratitude*, Melanie Klein stresses the fragmenting effect of greedy introjection. She writes:

> I found that concurrently with the greedy and devouring internalisation of the object – first of all the breast – the ego in varying degrees fragments itself and its object, and in this way achieves a dispersal of the destructive impulses and of the internal persecutory anxiety (1957, p. 191)

The patient's reaction to the failure of this greedy introjection and to the renewed internal persecution was one of despair and resulted in a temporary weakening of his drive toward integration and a very intense strengthening of his drive towards fragmentation, manifest in relinquishing his own jaw and the related functions of his ego, as well as a strong tendency to do the 'post-mortem' – that is, a complete fragmentation of his object and his ego.

The subsequent six months of analysis, made up of a nearly unremitting continuation of the type of resistance manifest on the Wednesday, has finally brought a clarification of his dread of a total psychotic collapse. Only through recent analysis of the mechanisms potentially responsible for this – namely the oral sadism and the omnipotent expulsive power of his eyes – has it been possible for a renewed approach to the depressive position to be made.

CHAPTER TWELVE

Repression, forgetting, and unfaithfulness[1]

(1974)

T he concept of repression winds its way throughout
the entire length of Freud's work, beginning with the
Studies in Hysteria and ending with 'Analysis termina-
ble and interminable'. At first he considered it to be equivalent
to the concept of defence, but later he differentiated between
repression as a specific mechanism and defence in the wider
category of defensive operations. In this process of subsum-
ing repression under the wider category, the concept tended
to get lost. Writing about it in the 1937 paper 'Analysis termi-
nable and interminable', Freud attempted to rescue it from
being overwhelmed by the other mechanisms that were being
described by various authors at the time. I do not wish here to
trace in any detail the ways in which Freud struggled to give
this important concept definitive form, the ways in which it
was linked to the libido theory, later in a sense 'sexualised' and
linked to the conflicts between male and female and between
active and passive, and finally, linked to anxiety when Freud
saw that anxiety was a motive force of repression and not a
consequence of its activity. Instead, I want to turn attention to

---

1 First published in the *Bulletin of the British Psychoanalytical Society*, 1974.

two more poetic statements of Freud's – one a very early statement in which he tried to find a model for the concept of the
transference, and one thirty years later, when he tried to use the
same model to describe the action of repression. I turn to these
more poetic statements because I think that in them we find
something of the clinician's vision, which is in the case of Freud
something very different from the theoretician's conceptions.

In 'Fragment from an analysis of a case of hysteria', Freud
writes:

> What are transferences? They are new editions or facsimiles
> of the impulses and phantasies which were aroused and made
> conscious during the process of analysis. But they have this
> peculiarity which is characteristic of their species – that they
> replace some earlier person by the person of the physician.
> To put it another way: a whole series of psychological experi-
> ences are reviewed, not as belonging to the past, but as applied
> to the person of the physician at the present moment. Some
> of these transferences have a content which differs from that
> of their model in no respect whatever except for substitution.
> These then, to keep to the same metaphor, are merely new
> impressions or reprints. Others are more ingeniously con-
> structed. Their content has been subjected to a moderating
> influence – to sublimation as I call it. And they may even
> become conscious by cleverly taking advantage of some real
> peculiarity in the physician's person or circumstances, and
> attaching themselves to that. These then will no longer be
> new editions but revised editions. (Freud, 1905e, p. 116)

I wish to draw attention to the 'cleverness' that Freud cites as
the foundation of these revised editions. By this he implies that
the past has been made acceptable by some modification of its
content. This tampering with the truth is emphasised again when
Freud returns to this analogy 31 years later in 'Analysis termi-
nable and interminable'. He writes:

> It was from one of these mechanisms, repression, that the
> study of neurotic process took its whole start. There was
> never any doubt that repression was not the only procedure
> which the ego could employ for its purposes. Nevertheless a
> repression is something quite peculiar, and is more sharply

differentiated from the other mechanisms than they are from one another. I should like to make this relation to the other mechanisms clear by an analogy, though I know that in these matters analogies never carry us very far. Let us imagine what might have happened to a book at a time when books were not printed in editions but were written out individually. Suppose that a book of this kind contained statements of a kind which in later times were regarded as undesirable, as for instance according to Robert Eisler (1929) the writings of Flavius Josephus must have contained passages about Jesus Christ which were offensive to later Christendom. At the present day the only defensive mechanism to which the official censorship could resort would be to confiscate and destroy every copy of the whole edition. At that time however various methods were used for making the book innocuous. One method would be for the offending passages to be thickly crossed through so that they were illegible. In that way the book could not be transcribed, and the next copyists of the book would produce a text which was unexceptionable but which had gaps in certain passages and so might be unintelligible in them. Another way, however, if the authorities were not satisfied with this but wished also to conceal any indication that the text had been mutilated, would be for them to proceed to distort the text. Single words would be left out or replaced by others and new sentences interpolated. Best of all the whole passage would be erased and a new one which said exactly the opposite set in its place. The next transcriber would then produce a text which would arouse no suspicion but was falsified. It no longer contained what the author wished to say. And it is highly probable that the corrections had not been made in the direction of truth. (Freud, 1937c, p. 236)

If we attempt to amalgamate these two statements using the same analogy – one a statement about the transference and the other a statement about repressions – what we have as a result is something that can be envisaged as a series of relationships, each a transference relationship and each involving a clever distortion of the truth of this primary model. From this point

of view the transference that we examine in the analytic situation would be seen as only the most recent transference event,
and one that would present as its content evidences of this serial
distortion of the primal relation that is being represented. The
process of reconstruction of the infantile relationships would
involve a whole series of revisions of bowdlerised history.

For this reason, and for many others of course, psychoanalysis has moved away from its early concern with reconstruction
and is now inclined to view the transference as being primarily
of interest because of its immediacy – that is, the immediate
evidence of infantile relationships to internal objects being
externalised onto the person of the analyst. Psychoanalysis is
not alone in taking this view of history: there are historians
who would also say that the writing of history is primarily an
activity of the imagination working in the present and utilising
events of the past for investigating manifestations of the present. It is on the basis of this view of history and of the analytic
process that I wish to discuss the mechanism of repression and
to describe its operation in unconscious phantasy, very much
in the way that Freud describes the activity of clever distortions
of the truth, producing 'revised editions' by means of mission
and interpolation.

I discuss it under four headings: 1) the content of the
repressed; 2) the mechanism of repression; 3) the return of the
repressed; 4) the economics of repression. In doing this, I try to
relate the operation of the mechanism to the analytic process in
its longitudinal aspect.

The content of the repressed

Clinical material no. 1

Shortly after a holiday break, and in expectation of a bill for the
previous month, somewhat troubled by the realisation that his
improved income implied the necessity to raise the low fee he
was paying to approximate to the analyst's regular fee, a patient
dreamt the following:

*He was upstairs in either the front or the back of a tram, and a gang
entered to rob a safe that seemed to be there. He felt he could either*

call for help and resist, or cooperate with them by allowing them to tie him up and knock him about a little. he decided on the latter course, thinking that perhaps he could get a share of the loot. Accordingly he allowed a tough fellow to knock him about and imprison him behind criss-cross aluminium bars (which reminded him of a piece of sculpture he had seen, called 'Unknown Political Prisoner'). After the thieves had gone, he extricated himself and went down to tell the conductor, who said 'The devils!' but showed no sympathy for the cut on the patient's cheek. At that moment he noticed a little Negro boy who was a favourite pupil of his, sitting with his father. But he could not remember the child's name; he introduced himself to the father by saying, 'I'm your child's teacher.' He awoke at that moment and could not remember the child's name until he was relating the dream in his session some hours later.

We already knew this 'gang' well from many dreams and knew its connection with the actual gang of semi-delinquents with whom the years of primary and secondary school had been spent. We knew how this 'gang' view of the world inspired in him an exploitative and insincere relation to the analyst as a member, or even leader, of a psychoanalytic gang: how it prevented his sexual relation with his wife from being tender, since he always had to be in a position of 'getting a piece' to boast about internally: how it stamped on his character generally a shallow, opportunistic and fraudulent quality. An 'unknown political prisoner', indeed!

What I wish to stress about the dream is the relation of the robbing of the safe and the loss from the patient's mind of the name of his favourite little boy pupil. The point is this: he allowed, and even connived in, the robbing of his good object – the breast, his analyst in regard to fees and cooperation – and as a result found himself identified with the robbed object in his own parental role toward his little pupil, empty-headed of the child's name. He is identified with an object that has lost its capacity to recognise a child as a unique individual, rather than merely 'my pupil', 'my child', 'my patient' – in a possessive and egocentric sense. It is an old accusation from his childhood that his parents exploited him in this way – that his mother showed him off, his father boasted of his talents. Later work in the analysis strongly suggested that he had misconstrued the quality of their pride and affection.

Discussion

Repression is a mechanism of defence that creates gaps in the availability of experiences for conscious recollection and reconstruction. These gaps result from an unconscious phantasy in which something – either an object or its contents – is lost, strayed, or stolen. The clinical consequences are either primary, due to the altered internal situation, or secondary, due to identification processes. In that sense they appear to be symptomatic or characterological. In the first instance gaps in memory result; in the second, defective capacity for recollection. In the example given, both of these consequences are manifest in the patient after he had awakened from the dream. In the first instance the content of his object, the names of the children, had been stolen, as shown by the defective conductor-daddy only referring to the gang as 'the devils' and ignoring the patient's cut cheek. The waking patient was then unable to remember either his little pupil's name or the name of the sculptor of the 'Unknown Political Prisoner'. But furthermore his identification with the defective object is manifested in the session by his attitude to his own inability to recollect these two names. In the dream he is content to cover the defect with 'I'm your little boy's teacher', and in the waking state to cover his defective relation to the sculptor with a vague reference to 'The Tate … Zadkin, or somebody'. He manifests unconcern about other people's individuality as an aspect of his character at this moment.

With regard to the primary defect of memory produced by an act of repression, the nature of the defect is distinctly different, depending on whether the lost, strayed, or stolen thing is an object or its content. Loss of an object produces a widespread and general amnesia for a whole *category of experiences* of the type represented by the relationship to that particular internal part- or whole-object; loss of an object's contents, on the other hand, produces amnesia only for specific events or facts.

The mechanism of repression

The circumstances of psychic structure that make repression possible are variable. The narcissistic organisation shown in this dream is most frequent. Weakness, neglect, apathy, or stupidity on the part of good parts of the self, both adult and infantile, are in evidence towards the delinquent and destructive parts.

In my experiences, the stolen, strayed, or lost object or attribute is invariably hidden or buried in the faeces (not the little Negro boy), whence it is in danger of being lost by anal expulsion into the outside world. This is the link between regression and manic mechanisms, with their characteristic denial of psychic reality, as described by Abraham ('Notes on manic-depressive insanity', 1911), and later in greater detail by Melanie Klein ('A contribution to the psychogenesis of manic-depressive states', 1935). The dread of losing good objects in this way poses a depressive problem that is very clearly seen in patients who have lost a parent in early life and retain little or no conscious memory of the relationship or person.

Clinical material no. 2

The approach of the Christmas holidays at the end of the first year in the analysis of an adolescent student was complicated by his having early on entered an agreement for a package tour, along with some friends, which would take him away for three weeks, missing the first two weeks of analysis in the new term. The consequence had been a series of anxiety dreams related to his sexual behaviour and possessiveness of his widowed mother, but his mind was utterly closed to the reconsideration of his plans.

In the last week of the analysis before the holiday he brought a dream: *There were some moths, and he wondered if they were British or had been bred abroad. They seemed either wax- or flesh-coloured, and he felt troubled by them in some way. But his professor said, 'Don't worry. Put them in a capsule (you know, like they did with the Beatles records – a time capsule, Music of the 1960s) and bury them somewhere. Then forget about them. You can always dig them up later.'*

He knew that the analyst, like his own parents and he himself, in fact, had been 'bred abroad' and could easily see that the moths referred to 'moth-er' and to the butterfly on the lampshade of the consulting room. he admired his professor but was suspicious of his being universally liked. He had studied the man's charm and had found it partly to consist of never hurting people's feelings by disagreeing or criticising. He somehow always seemed to agree, even though he sometimes subtly altered the other person's meaning in restatement. The father, who died when the patient was in latency, was also very charming, but the patient had long associated his mother's affectionate appellation of 'Hon', short for 'Honey', to 'Hun', the term used for the German in the First world War. He felt a similar suspicion towards the analyst as a father, while already clearly possessively attached to the analysis as a mothering situation. In his memory, the years prior to his father's death were relatively empty and the few recollections lacked vividness, markedly in contrast to the vibrant and full recall of the years immediately following.

After the dream was interpreted – a 'beautiful interpretation', he said – the recollection of early separation from his mother flooded his associations in vivid detail. From the age of five, he had been sent to 'camp', as was the custom in his parents' circle, for three weeks each summer up to the time of his father's death. These excursions had been a torment to him of loneliness and anxiety, tantrums and weeping, until he learned to 'forget about' his mother, probably under the tuition of an elder cousin.

Discussion

The dream shows with some brilliance the mechanism of this 'forgetting'. His internal mother was protectively encapsulated and buried in his faeces, under the direction of a destructive and tricky part – 'cousin' – of himself, not yet clearly differentiated from the rival professor Hun father. The danger to the mother in this procedure is explicitly denied but revealed in the uncertainty between 'wax' and 'flesh' colour of the moths. The danger of loss is similarly denied in the assumption that 'you can always dig them up later', but the injunction 'forget about them' may also, after all, include forgetting that you buried them at all, or ever possessed them.

It is clear that the patient has been driven to act out an early anxiety situation with the aim of obviating separation anxiety in relation to the external object (mother-analyst) by repression of the relationship. The dream shows the dynamics of the repression and also the latent anxiety consequences that had been adumbrated in the earlier series of anxiety dreams. Again the narcissistic organisation is evident (the bad cousin-professor) and shows how inadequate splitting-and-idealisation (confusion between the father and the bad cousin part of the self) contributes to the strength of the defensive tendencies.

However, it is of interest to note how different is the 'repressed' in the two cases mentioned: how much more primitive and pathological is the first instance than the second. There the primal good object is being robbed of its contents, with the result that the patient suffers a general defect in his mental capacities – i.e. to remember the names of his pupil-children, in identification with the damaged mother-breast. In the second case the object itself is being carefully buried-in-the-faeces with the consequent capacity for repression of the specific relationship, to be able to forget that particular object in the outside world, i.e. the analyst-mother, when he is on holiday.

The struggle set in motion by this piece of analytic work was particularly illuminating as the patient became distressingly aware of his reluctance to miss the two weeks of analysis but yet could not find the strength in himself to face the expected mockery from his friends in the event of his withdrawing from the group agreement.

The return of the repressed

In both cases events in psychic reality producing repression were set in motion by a decision. In both cases this decision involved a breach of fidelity to the good object, a retreat from depressive anxieties in a conflict situation. Although the ego of the first patient is clearly more primitive and the objects more partial, the events more subject to the use of projective identification (inside the tram), and the narcissism based on a more primitive form of sadism and aggression, both conflicts hang upon the balance of Ps↔D (Bion), that is, between paranoid-schizoid and depressive value systems in the object relations. I am suggesting that indeed the mechanism of repression teeters upon the knife-edge of sparing-the-self vs. sparing-the-object mental pain; and thus it has already come a long way from the more abandonedly destructive schizoid mechanisms such as splitting processes and massive projective identification.

Recovery of lost objects, bits of objects, and contents of objects from the faeces is a depressive task which must be performed for the self by good objects when the self rejects the mental pain of longing, guilt, remorse. This state of rejection is manifest in relation to gaps in the memory by dismissal of the problem. The recovery of lost dreams during an analytic session, either by effort on the patient's part out of concern for the work, or spontaneously during the session as a result of the analyst's work, is the most common realisation of this balanced situation.

Clinical material no. 3

A young woman, whose analysis had only recently broken through a severe impasse at the threshold of the depressive position, returned to the Monday session in a mood of aloofness, self-pity, evasion of responsibility, and abandonment to nymphomania phantasies, in all of which her disturbed little boy was the chief persecutor and fountainhead of her misery. The retreat into this state not only evaded the intense loneliness at infantile levels related to the weekend break, but also avoided the problem at an adult level of continuing the education she had abandoned some years earlier for a hasty and early marriage. This problem related to her early betrayal of her parents by disappointing them at school, always showing promise with her unusual talents and intelligence, only to throw away each opportunity by indolence.

    She dreamed on Saturday night that *there was a dead girl who might have been murdered by the patient's little boy, and to protect him she was burying the body, covering it lightly with soil. The head, however, seemed separate from. the body and was shaped like a ball. But then it seemed that there was a second body and that the crime consisted not in causing the deaths but in concealing the first one.*

    During the weekend the boy had been annoying the cat by kicking his new ball at it. The patient had confiscated the ball and at first thrown it into the garden, but then, fearing it might deflate in the cold, she had hidden it in the house. In the morning, after the dream, she could not remember where she had hidden it. The body she connected with her brother-in-law's favourite calendar of a nude girl painted with gold, which he affectionately called 'the finest brain in England'. In fact, one of the patient's friends, the 'finest brain' she knew, had been taken to hospital suddenly before the weekend.

After the dream and its related material had been interpreted, the patient acknowledged that, quite unlike weekends in the previous two months of the recent holiday, she had not thought of the analysis once during the separation and had felt reluctant to come to the session that day. As the warmth returned to the transference relationship during the session, she felt very weepy as thoughts turned to her father's early death.

The economics of repression and return

When the object has been buried in the faeces, its safety is always very precarious because of the danger of inadvertent anal expulsion. This is increased, of course, by the working of the repression, which induces forgetfulness of both the object itself and of the desire to preserve it for future recovery. To this source of insecurity there is added a manic trend towards expulsion of the object, in defence against the guilt coming from two sources – the unfaithfulness on the one hand, and the joylessness of the object's existence in the faeces on the other.

But one can see that a consortium of defensive tendencies of this type finds very little opposition unless the guilt is backed by an awareness of need for the object. If love were strong enough, the defences would never have been set in motion in the first place. But being a rather sophisticated defensive system mobilised by well-organised aspects of the infantile personality, it has an association with arrogance and ideas of independence that deny need for the object. Thus in the struggle from narcissistic organisation towards object relations, progress in respect of the problem of repression as an aspect of character is only made when the process has gone some considerable distance and reached what I have described as the 'threshold of the depressive position'.

Clinical material no. 4

A middle-aged man who had undertaken analysis because of a lack of achievement in his business had come gradually to realise the pathological significance and compulsive structure of his promiscuity and unfaithfulness. Three years of work had shown the narcissistic organisation, which consisted of an arrogant anal and phallic sadistic 'Negro' aspect of the infantile structures who seduced and dominated the little-boy part, some-times with threats but more often with promises of worldly gain and sensual gratification, a bit in the style of Mephistopheles with Faust. This representation derived its form from a period of homosexual submission in early puberty to an older Negro man, who used to take him to football games, a companionship earlier enjoyed with his deceased father.

During the third year of the analysis some gains had been made with regard to unfaithfulness to his wife and in resist-ing the opportunist trends in his behaviour. This advance was accompanied by dreams of mounting resistance to the influence of the 'Negro'. On the night before the last session prior to the Christmas break, he dreamed that *he was cycling with a black briefcase under his arm, but it slipped out and seemed to become somehow attached to the back wheel, so that it was dragged along the ground. He went on, looking back occasionally to see that it was still there. Then he was going past the football stadium, and rowdy crowds were coming out. A Negro and another man began to molest him, and he fought back. At a pause in the fighting, however, he thought of a better course, since the violence had gone out of the conflict. He took an Atlas from the briefcase. This he showed to the two assailants, who were very interested in the maps.*

His association to the Atlas was 'Charles Atlas', the strong man whose ads he had been so impressed by in his youth – 'You can have a body like mine', or some such thing. It was clear that the briefcase represented the faeces containing the dead father, who was only resurrected from his precarious position when the patient became aware of the need for an ego-ideal with whom to identify. It is of great interest that this identification was not of a projective sort, with the powerful body for the purpose of defeating his attackers, but an introjective one with the persua-sive salesman aspect of the father, who was interested in helping boys develop their bodies and minds. Following the elucidation of the dream, the patient began to weep, mainly about his wife going to the States to visit her parents, occasions previously of secret satisfaction and promiscuous intentions for my patient. But he was also aware that he was unhappy about the break in the analysis. This was a very marked shift from his former manic flights from separation pain in the transference.

Summary

We set out to rescue the concept of repression from an oblivion to which Freud's shift from libido theory, with its energetics model, to structural theory, with its emphasis on integration, seemed inevitably to consign it. In order to carry out this rescue, we attempted to show that the phenomenology of forgetfulness, particularly of a type that can be related directly to unfaithfulness to love objects, could best be understood in terms of the concept of repression when it was seen to act in a structural rather than in a cathectic manner. We tried to relate this point of view to the poetic analogies Freud had used, both early and late in his career, to describe the working of repression.

The main body of the paper consisted of four clinical examples by means of which we tried to exemplify a number of points: that repression comes into play in relation to the phenomenology of forgetfulness and unfaithfulness fairly late in the analytic process, at the threshold of the depressive position; that the mechanism operates through the unconscious phantasy of an object, whole or part, or its contents being lost, strayed, or stolen and buried in the faeces; that this carries a danger of inadvertent manic expulsion of the objet; that a recovery of the lost object tends to depend upon the service of a good external object, unless the person can feel the need for recovery of the object to reinforce the impact of regret and guilt in moving the subject towards the depressive position.

Conclusions

By tracing Freud's use of a poetic image – the reprinting and revising of editions of books – from its early use describing the transference, forward 32 years to its subsequent use to describe repression. I have attempted to create a background in his thought for a modern use of the term 'repression' in the context of clinical work carried on within a structure of theory. What could only be thought of as a useful analogy in earlier days can now be given a certain concreteness in our mode of thought, even though our theory is no more than a model. The concrete object, the book, of Freud's analogy now becomes the concrete internal object, which is manipulated in psychic reality through the means of omnipotence generated in the narcissistic organisation.

In the first example, the manipulation appears to be exclusively contained within the dream of 'sharing the loot', and only the consequences of this 'cleverness' can be found in the patient's relations in the outside world, as manifest in forgetting the names of his pupils and in his characteristic indifference to the accuracy of his recollections. But in both the second and third examples, the cleverness has involved the acting-out part of the process – the holiday trip in the second example and the throwing out and hiding the ball in the third. In all three cases the attack is upon the maternal transference relationship, mainly at the part-object level of the breast, and represents a clever attempt to obviate the emotional cost of that object by seeking, by one means or other, to enjoy its benefits when it is present without suffering pain in separation. The fourth example is at a more whole-object level.

These four examples, by focusing on the momentary functioning of the mechanism of repression in the transference, demonstrate its operation in detail, so that one can appreciate that, while the wish to forget may be conscious, the mechanism of repression is totally unconscious, insofar as it consists of an infantile phantasy of violence and hiding the *corpus delicti* or its stolen or lost contents in the faeces. This distinction between the wish and the mechanism has been overlooked by critics of Freud's modes of thought, especially by philosophers (eg. Wittgenstein, Hamlyn) who tend to accuse him of equivocation.

In closing this paper, I wish to make clear that I do not think that repression is the only, or even the main, mechanism operative in defects of memory. It is a relatively sophisticated mechanism, closely related to depressive conflicts, and it appears in analysis as an important factor in defensive operations in the transference only after more primitive mechanisms such as splitting and projective identification have been greatly lessened. I do not think that it accounts for the so-called 'infantile amnesia'.

CHAPTER THIRTEEN

The role of pregenital confusions in erotomania[1]

(1974)

When Mrs R first came to analysis, she was disquieted mainly by evidences of an inexplicable coldness and brutality, which burst out at her children, a boy and girl, whose development seemed in many ways unsatisfactory. But in the course of a difficult analysis and against great resistance, the idealisation of her husband and their marriage broke down and revealed a floridly perverse relationship of which she played the willing slave to his genius, obsessionality, and selfishness. As she gradually disengaged herself from this, the relationship became insupportable, and they agreed to stay together for the children's sake alone. Through this four-year period the analytic situation forged slowly ahead in the face of a strongly erotic transference and intense voyeurism, which gradually revealed an infantile situation of fusion with a parental couple related to sharing the parental bedroom during her breastfeeding period. this generated a strongly blissful state of mind, which resisted interpretation, but when it yielded on occasions, evidences appeared of a brutal wilfulness

---

1   Presented to the British Psychoanalytic Society, 1974; first published in *Sincerity: Collected Papers of Donald Meltzer,* ed. A. Hahn (Karnac, 1994).

and independence of judgement covered by surface compliance. This period of stress during which a change of house, removal from the parental bedroom, weaning, toilet training. and the birth of a baby sister, had followed hard upon the heels of one another.

As these transference configurations were worked through in the next year, Mrs R began to feel that the end of the analysis was in sight, and a tentative date was mooted. She then fell passionately in love with a man she had known but hardly noticed for many years, and she set about winding up her marriage in the expectation of consummating this new relationship once she was free. She now felt quite strong and independent, and a date of termination was set for the following summer. But no sooner was this agreed in principle than a distinct change became noticeable in her states of mind in and out of the analysis. Erotomania seemed to invade her new relationship, while a certain conspiratorial and brutal attitude began to spoil the orderly disengagement from her husband.

At the same time her relationship to the analyst became patronising; doubt and even contempt invaded her feelings about the earlier analytic work, and she began to insist that she had to terminate forthwith for lack of money. When this was discounted as a motive, she agreed to continue on the grounds that the discussions with the analyst helped her to manage the relationship with her children in this critical and delicate period. At times her dominance seemed to threaten to destroy her new love relation, but for her lover's strength and patience.

During this period, in the face of contempt and coldness, a poverty of material and the constant threat of interruption, a particular formulation could nonetheless be constructed and tightened by each new piece of material. The formulation was to this effect: unlike her weaning in childhood, which had produced a splitting of a horizontal sort in which her relationship to the breast was relinquished in favour of a secret and perverse preoccupation with her faeces idealised variously as food, penis, and babies, she was now turning away from the breast in the father's penis and entering into a fierce competition for control and possession of that object: thus invoking a confusion between nipple-in-mouth and penis-in-vagina to obviate the experience of weaning and relinquishment. But Mrs R was adamant: she could now spare the analyst only two hours a week and would miss the first week after the Easter holiday to visit her lover.

She returned cold and aloof, but to our surprise a rich yield of material followed in the next two weeks, which broke into the acting-out and brought things under control once more. The night after the first session, she dreamed that *she and her lover were invited to dinner by a couple who were his best friends, but instead of eating, they were embracing at the table. Then it seemed to have just been a dream that she awakened from to find herself in bed with her husband, and she felt repelled by his advances.* She awoke in great distress but was relieved to realise it had all been a dream. She then returned to sleep, only to have an even more upsetting dream, in which *she and another woman were in rivalry for her lover, lying in bed on either side of him. She was horrified to see that both had dark erect penises instead of nipples.* Mrs R associated this with the fact that her mother's nipples are in fact dark and had been erect on every occasion she could remember having seen them. This dream seemed to indicate the state of projective identification and confusion of identity in which the baby felt herself in rivalry with the mother for the father. It demonstrated the nipple-penis confusion involved in the erotisation of the breast.

At the end of that session Mrs R said that she felt it unbearable to continue without payment and would prefer to stop. The analyst indicated that these dreams made him more willing to agree, but that his own preference was unequivocally on the side of trying to bring the analysis to a proper termination. The following session she brought a dream again: *She was warning her children to stay away from the hive of dormant bees that her cousin Doris (who figured in the analysis as the friend who had taught her about sex and masturbation in puberty) had given her, but the children paid no heed. The bees awoke, buzzing angrily, and the patient shouted to the children to run, and then awoke.* This seemed an encouraging dream, an improved differentiation of adult from infantile levels and an awareness that infantile masturbation was related to rage at being disturbed and awakened from sleep by parental sexuality (referring to the dreams of the previous session).

Mrs R seemed shocked by the dream she brought to the next session, for it seemed so strongly to confirm the formulation of her brutal treatment of her husband and contempt for his penis. In the dream *a dog was lying whimpering on the ground beside a bitch in heat, who finally allowed him to mount her. But his penis grew huge and human and then metamorphosed into an idiot boy covered with semen who came, to Mrs R's horror, to embrace her.* Mrs R commented that she had always found her husband's semen very repulsive, but felt quite different with her lover.

She began to understand the brutal aspect of the erotomania and its foundation in competition with the mother for control of the father's penis and how this linked with her former outbreaks of brutality to the children. A definite softening now appeared in the transference and brought the first renewed flush of trust and good feeling towards the analyst. That night she dreamed that *an American man was trying to persuade her to take part in an experiment at her mother's home, to which she finally agreed, but sceptically. It was to take place in the garage and involved wearing earphones. When she returned to the kitchen, Mrs R was shocked to see two prostitutes lying on the kitchen table, dressed but clearly awaiting coitus. She took her little girl aside and told her not to look.*

This dream seemed to suggest the following optimistic interpretation: the analyst-daddy (American man) was finally succeeding in persuading this little girl to try the experiment of living outside her mother's body and identity (the garage) in order that her sleep might be in contact with her internal objects in an auditory way as in analysis (the earphones), instead of being disturbed (like the angry bees) by the sight of the parental intercourse externally (in bed with mummy and daddy and in competition with that 'other' woman). That only drives her into a narcissistic organisation (with Doris, who teachers her about sex and masturbation) and interferes with her recognition of the difference between adult and infantile (herself and her daughter) and thus weakens the ability to understand and protect children from the brutality that is linked to erotomania – the bitch in heat.

CHAPTER FOURTEEN

The relation of splitting of attention to splitting of self and objects[1]

(1981)

Although the delineation of splitting-and-idealisation as an essential step in early development found its place in Melanie Klein's theories of development quite soon in her researches, it was only with the 1946 paper 'Notes on some schizoid mechanisms' that the wide variety of splitting processes, normal and pathological, came under systematic scrutiny. The use of splitting processes in the sense of constructive differentiation as against their use for breaking links in the service of defence found repeated expression in the literature of the 1950s and 1960s. But Wilfred Bion's description of processes of attention and their relation to thinking in *Attention and Interpretation* (1970) marked the beginning of a new dimension of investigation of the modes of operation of splitting processes. Those who had followed Melanie Klein's way of thinking – her implicit model of the mind, that is – assumed that splitting processes operated by unconscious phantasy, implemented by omnipotence, effecting concrete alterations in the structure of self and objects in psychic reality. Bion's extension of Kleinian mechanisms to an arena of operation on mental functions as

1 First published in *Contemporary Psychoanalysis*, 17:232-238 (1981).

well as mental structures revealed a new level of phenomenology in the consulting-room.

This paper is intended as an illustration of how these two
levels of splitting processes can operate in parallel and potenti-
ate one another's impact on mental states. The exposition will
be confined to a single piece of rather intricate clinical material,
for which a considerable amount of background in the psychoanalytical process is required to consolidate the credibility of
the interpretation being put forward.

A young man of twenty-one entered analysis two and a half
years following his failure to achieve satisfactory enough results
in his A-level exams to obtain a place at Oxford. Six months of
depressed indolence had followed this disappointment, the therapy
for which was a working visit to his godparents in another country.
There he had seemed to fare well for the first half year, living in
their house and working in their factory, until he was asked to
move out for a month to make room for some of their married
children come visiting. This had initiated a quietly delusional
state with severe anxiety of being 'thrown away' accompanied by a
frantic increase in his diligence and almost complete cessation of
eating. Padding his clothing and seclusiveness succeeded in hiding
his deteriorating state until he was so emaciated and weak that
he could hardly stand. Six months after his physical recovery he
started analysis and had completed the first year at the time of
this material. His illness proved to be a long-standing confusional
state based on massive projective identification which, prior to the
eruption of severe anxiety, had mainly shown itself in his character structure. He was an unusual boy, rather babyish-looking
thanks to a large head and puppy fat. Very high intelligence had
enabled him to excel effortlessly at school through docility to his
persecutors but he was fairly unsocialised, cynically critical and
dissatisfied and without genuine interests of his own. For instance
an extraordinary competence in music, both instrumental and
theoretical had been achieved purely on the basis of feeling that
he had been designated the musical genius of the five variously
talented children of distinguished parents.

The patient's confusional state (a 'geographical psychosis'
which I have described in some detail elsewhere) manifested
itself in his picture of the world in which he lived, or was, rather,

imprisoned. It characteristically consisted of three different areas with differing characteristics: his room, an erotic mastur-bation chamber; his place of work, a slave-labour camp; and the consulting room, a place of light and air looking out on a happy and free world that he could not reach. These three areas, corresponding in meaning to the internal mother's vagina, rectum and head-breast respectively, were connected by the city of Oxford with its tortuous alleys filled with hostile university students through which he had to cycle with eyes on the ground (the mother›s intestine) snatching a bit of food from a small shop en route. His relation to food as stolen bits of faeces was the main focus of the analytical work in the first six months and seemed to eventuate in his emergence from the claustrum.

The consequent change in his state of mind was fairly dramatic. A frantic hunger of the mind replaced the furtive hunger for food, but he soon discovered that the analysis alone did not satisfy this craving. Ambition and competitiveness, particularly with his older brother and his distinguished father, and with his analyst and the male patients who preceded and followed him at his sessions, began to obsess him. He began reading literature and psychoanalytic literature as well, but soon discovered that his capacity for concentration was greatly interfered with. His atten-tion would be drawn away to ruminations of a mathematical sort, or phantasies in which he was carrying on a scathing commentary on a football game, or on the commentator who was reporting a football game, or on himself for commenting on the commentator's comments on the game. This began to invade the analytic situation as well, so that he would fall silent, or break off listening during interpretive work by the analyst. Furthermore his dreams, which had been so illuminating to the work, dried up and his plans for resuming his education came to a standstill.

In this context a breakthrough occurred which was set in motion by an intrusion on the analytical process. A seminar given weekly by the analyst in the local child guidance clinic had been moved to the new hospital where the patient worked as supplies clerk. The knowledge that the analyst was in the hospital on Tuesday afternoon, and actually seeing him enter on one occasion, disturbed the patient in ways that quite surprised him, for the eruption of jealousy of the people who attended the seminar was unmistakeable. In the third week of this intrusive change in routine dreams broke through and revealed the nature of the transference situation on the very eve of his twenty-second birthday.

To the fourth session of the week he brought the following dream, very pleased to be able to do so: *there were three buildings arranged on three sides of a square. One was a very dilapidated warehouse with one broken window, a broken glass canopy over its front door from which a ramp descended. The second was the canteen of the old hospital filled with people, and the third was long and narrow like a Nissen hut or a train, and he was in it seated at a table as in an inter-city train. From the window of the warehouse, which now seemed to be a maternity hospital, a huge object resembling a furniture castor was thrown. It rolled down the ramp, seemed to threaten to invade the canteen but finally collapsed like a spent top in front of the train-building. Then two youths appeared from the warehouse-maternity hospital, the smaller looking a typical 'middle-class swat', and four or five men in hospital porters coats came out to surround him. But to the delight of the people in the canteen, the boy of perhaps eight or ten years hit one and knocked him out. But they were less pleased when he commenced kicking him with his 'Doc Miller' boots (a type of heavy work shoe worn by aggressive youths, but similar to the ones recently worn by the patient to replace the tattered suede shoes of the early months of the analysis). Furthermore the boy kept taunting the fallen porter, saying, 'Do you like that, Andrew?' and 'How does that feel, Andrew?' Then the train-building where the patient was seated began to move over the countryside, which seemed diagramatic, with rather toy-like farms and houses. At one house they pass, he could see the boy's mother on the telephone to the porter's mother defending her boy on the grounds that he›s been provoked.*

The patient immediately recognises that the 'Doc Miller' boots referred to the analyst's initials and it was suggested that this kicking represented an aggressive use of interpretation. He agreed that he had been doing this in fact in his mind lately, replacing his old vocabulary of contempt with a new one derived from psycho-analese. It also reminded him of the time at age sixteen when he had actually struck his father and in fact knocked him out. But he could think of no one named Andrew. It was suggested that it might be a pun, the four or five porters being the *hand* that *drew* him out of the mother's body, first of all at his birth, whose anniversary was approaching, and in the analysis. Perhaps this was the thanks the father-doctor gets for bringing the baby out of its dilapidated womb into a world where it has to 'swat' in order to develop. But it seemed that some differentiation between that baby and an adult observing and thinking part of his mind now existed, a part that was eager for development, perhaps another pun on *training*. Was the boy who had never had any interests of his own beginning to form an ambition to train as a psychoanalyst. The patient confessed that this was in his mind and that he had recently found himself watching how the analyst operated. The analyst further suggested that this castor-like object looked like the placenta, but this did not seem to enlighten anything. But the patient added that he had recently been looking at a book about childbirth in which it was mentioned that animals eat the placenta and perhaps human mothers should do likewise.

This brought to a close that day's investigation. Its harvest had been a bit of a surprise to both of us, revealing so clearly the area of infantile resentment over being drawn forth from a world of slavery and seclusiveness into one of work and development, a 'provocation' with regard to which the mother was felt to be in sympathy with the baby. But perhaps most interesting to the analyst was the evidence of the 'Doc Miller' boots, with their implication of wishing to learn the father's skills in order to use them against him aggressively, to 'draw forth' from the symbolic representations their meaning and forge them into weapons for control, tyranny, revenge. It was in line with this aspect that the dream of Friday did not come as so complete a surprise.

The patient started the Friday session in fact in a state of somewhat sullen inhibition of thought, but after two minutes he suddenly remembered the dream from the night before which he had awakened from at about four in the morning and then returned to sleep. In this dream *it seemed that he and another man had been ordered to decapitate two people. The one that fell to him was a small boy who seemed quite resigned to the event, which was to take place in the mud of a unmade-up alley, his head resting on the edge of one of the ruts. But that seemed not to be satisfactory so the scene shifted to a small corridor down which he wheeled the boy on a strange trolley to a room with a window looking out on playing fields. There he took his curved Turkish sword to do the job, but, feeling unwilling, he kept missing the neck. And as he did so, the boy seemed to gain some resistance to being beheaded and began to avoid the stroke as well. Eventually a Negro 'dressed as a doctor' entered and put an end to the game by lowering a bar (like the bar which ends the game in slot-machine snooker tables by preventing the balls from rolling down into the tray). But he also pointed out the window for the patient to notice what was going on there. In fact he realised at that point that he had been partly watching all the time he was 'beheading' the boy and had seen the following process: on one field there was a football game and on the other a cricket match. Because a girl had joined the football game, most of the boys had left in protest to go to queue for bowling in the cricket.*

The dream seemed all too clear to both analyst and patient to require much association. It told the story of how he renders himself mindless by watching phantasy football and cricket games and carrying on a subsidiary game of commentary and anti-commentary. Why the analyst should be represented as a Negro was puzzling, but it was clear that the hand which had drawn him forth from his claustrum had also lowered the bar on his ruminative mindlessness. But it was not clear who had ordered this beheading nor why its implementation was so docilely effected by both executioner and victim alike. Some hint came when the question was raised about the 'curved Turkish sword'. The patient reported that at the moment of telling the dream he had been unable to think of the word 'scimitar'. It is a car model that he much admires but remembers that when he first saw the analyst's Volvo SE he had thought it superior and that all Scimitar owners would now be buying the Volvo instead, although it was clearly a copy. In fact the Reliant Scimitar used to be a four-door saloon until they copied the Volvo and changed it into a sports estate car, when it achieved its present popularity.

So there would seem to be a hidden link between the two dreams, distinguishing between ambition that grows out of envy and that which springs from admiration and gratitude. The little boy whose mother excuses his aggressive behaviour in knocking out his father on the grounds that he was provoked has used the 'Doc Miller' interpretations as the patient has used the scimitar interpretations, for aggressive splitting processes, in the first instance on his object, splitting the one finger-porter from the others of the hand that drew him forth, in the second instance on his own mind, to destroy his capacity for observation and thought.

But notice also that what has been split is his attention, for while he is attending to the beheading he is also watching the transactions on the playing fields, just as the patient reports that while listening to the analyst's interpretations he has also been watching his method of operation as the first step in his psycho-analytical training. It is of some interest that the landscape of the first dream may have a reference, with its neat toy-like fields, farms and houses to the waiting room of the analytic suite. This room is equipped also to be used as a playroom for child therapy, and has a lino marked in squares of tiles; on one occasion there was a plastic bowl of toys left by mistake on the table.

Material as rich as this lends itself clearly to almost endless investigation, but for the purpose of this brief paper it seems best to concentrate on the obtrusive item of the parallel processes of splitting self and object and splitting of attention. It raises the provocative question of the nature of *interest*. It is a very major aspect of this patient's character disorder that he has never been able to form *his own* interests but has, out of the sort of docility exemplified in the beheading-dream, pursued the activities he felt bid to by his persecutors, mainly internal but confused with his father as an external autocrat (which in fact I think he probably is not). It is not clear whether we should take *interest* merely to signify that which is the object of attention or rather to take *attention* to be that state which manifests interest. Perhaps we would do best to think of it both ways in different circumstances: of attention and interest being mental functions which can be deployed to objects; but also of objects having qualities whose apprehension can attract interest and attention. Where the thirst for knowledge is strong the mind must surely actively seek objects to which it can fruitfully deploy its interest and attention, while weak or inhibited epistemophilic instinct would wait in relative passivity to have its interest and attention attracted or aroused. In either case the nature of the objects of interest and attention would differ depending on whether the mind is in a state corresponding to paranoid-schizoid or depressive position, dangerous objects in the former and beautiful objects in the latter being most charismatic. But the material here presented suggests a third and clinically important category of objects to which attention may be deployed: uninteresting objects, represented here by the transactions on the playing fields.

Adhesive identification[1]

(1974)

This process of 'adhesive identification' that I am going to describe is something Esther Bick and I began working on in our own separate ways and talking about together back in the early 1960s after Melanie Klein's death. We were both terribly lonely, since the person who had been carrying the load was now gone. Somebody, everybody, had to pick up the bit of it that he could carry. During that time Esther Bick was working in various ways. First of all she introduced infant observation into the curriculum of the Tavistock Clinic training for child psychotherapists, and in the Institute of Psychoanalysis. She was also treating some psychotic patients, children, and supervising the treatment of a large number of children. I remember there came a period when she kept saying to me, 'Oh, I don't know how to talk about it, they are just like that' (sticking her hands together). 'It is something different.' I did not know what she was talking about for a long time. I myself at that time was doing my ordinary practice, which is a mixture of neurotic patients, training cases, one or two schizophrenic patients, a few children,

---

1 Shortened version of a talk at the White Institute in 1974, first published in *Contemporary Psychoanalysis* 11(3): 289-310 (1975).

and supervising a lot of work with children. I began to find things with autistic children that were also like something stuck together. Gradually we came to something that we think is new and interesting, but in order to understand it, one has to go back to history, and that is what I want to do now.

Identification processes seem to me to have a very funny place in Freud's writings. As phenomena, he seems to have been very brilliant in observing them; they are mentioned even in *Studies in Hysteria*. 'Elizabeth' was identified with her mother and her father. 'Dora' was identified. The 'Rat Man' was identified. You hear this over and over again, as having something to do with imitation and vaguely to do with character. Then he came to the *Leonardo* paper. Although it is not a nice paper at all from the point of view of art history, it does seem to me to be important from the point of view of psychoanalytic history, because it is the first time that Freud takes a life and tries to understand it as a whole thing: to separate the pathology from a matrix of health and life processes. Health did not seem to interest him very much. In his early writings he seems to be purely a psychopathologist and you might say, not interested in people. The *Leonardo* paper starts something different: there he speaks of identification processes in a meaningful way that is connected with the beginnings of a concept of narcissism; and he states that there is something he would like to call 'narcissistic identifications'. In his paper on the 'Wolf Man' also, Freud seems to recognise narcissistic identifications and to realise that they have something to do with identity and distortions of identity.

Then suddenly, Freud begins to take an interest in the ideal ego and the ego-ideal; and then finally, in the 1920s, the superego. The concept of identification comes to be used in a very different way. Using Ferenczi's terms, he speaks of introjection into the ego and the establishment of a gradient within the ego by which a portion of it is separated off as the superego, and this he calls an identification. That is very puzzling because it seems to set up an internal voice, an observing function, a part of the ego that now observes and criticises the ego. He seems quickly to forget the other ego ideal function – that is, of encouraging and supporting the ego – in favour of its harsher, more restrictive and punitive aspects. Somehow this conceptual use of the term 'identification' for the process by which the superego is established does not seem to fit with the phenomenological use of the term as used in the case histories, as a type of imitation. To judge from the papers on the anal character and 'Some Character Types Met with in Analytic Work', Freud's idea of character still seems bound to the libido theory and the ways in which libido is diverted, inhibited, sublimated, reacted against, and so on. His idea was that character is build up through the management of the vicissitudes of instinct.

This has puzzled me for years. If you compare Freud's paper on *Mourning and Melancholia* with Abraham's paper on melancholia and manic-depressive states, you can see an important difference in the kind of models they had in mind. Freud gets into a terrific muddle about who is abusing whom: is the ego ideal abusing the ego? Is the ego abusing this object that has been taken inside? Whereas Abraham is quite clear about it and speaks in very concrete terms. He says that an object has been attacked internally and turned into faeces; it has then been defaecated out and then compulsively reintrojected by a process that has the meaning of eating the faeces, and this faecal object becomes established internally. Freud could never have talked in this way, and for a very important reason. He could not get rid of the preconceptions of the neurophysiological sort on the one hand and the so-called hydrostatic model of instinct on the other in order to conceptualise the mind as a place, a space. Nowhere in his writings is there a conceptualisation of spaces. He comes a little closer to it in the Schreber case when he talks about the world destruction phantasy and about what world was destroyed – inner or outer – but then he hedges it in a very peculiar way and says that it was a world that had been built up through the precipitate of identifications. He uses the words 'identifications' and 'sublimations'. I have never understood what he meant by that. He speaks of the world as having fallen to pieces by the withdrawal of libido, as if a kind of magnet could draw the mortar out from within the bricks and the thing would just collapse. But in a footnote, in which he quotes Heine's poem, he makes it quite clear that it has been *smashed* to pieces: it has not just crumbled from neglect or withdrawal of interest.

I think Freud had difficulty in shifting to a model in which the inside of the mind was a place where things could really happen and not just be imagined. This term 'imagined' is not good enough to describe the events of the mind. It fudges the issue and does not account for the relentlessness and inevitability with which events follow one another, particularly the inevitability with which attacks on these objects, damaging them, produce psychopathological changes that have really to be painfully repaired and restored in order for the process of recovery to take place.

This is where Freud was and remained until the end of his life. In the 1920s when Melanie Klein began to work with children, and was studying with Abraham, Abraham almost immediately began to hear about a very special space experienced by these children in a very concrete way, inside themselves and in particular inside their mothers' bodies. This evidence had not really been unavailable to Freud, because Little Hans talked about the same things: about the time when his little sister Hanna was inside the stork box, and the box was inside the carriage, which was obviously his mother. And it was closely connected with his fear of loaded wagons falling over, and the relationship of the horse to the wagon, and so on. Freud saw all that quite clearly but *he did not take any interest in it.* He took no interest at all in Little Hans's proliferation of fantasy about the time before Hanna was born, and the time before he was born – when he and Hanna were together in the stork box, the things they did, the things they ate, the places they went, and so on. Freud sweeps all of that aside and attributes it to his pulling his father's leg and taking revenge on him because of the stork story, as if to say 'If you expect me to believe the stork story, you've got to believe this rubbish.' This was the evidence that Mrs Klein did not sweep aside, and which put her onto this whole question of spaces: spaces inside the self, spaces inside objects, and a place where concrete things happened that had relentless and evident consequences and could be studied as part of the transference process.

To me this is really a major move, and it was from the study of processes of phantasy related to these spaces that our concepts of the pregenital Oedipus complex and the concreteness of internal objects – the prelude to the genital Oedipus complex, part-object relationships, and so on – originate. All the work she produced in the 1930s stemmed from this, and was very controversial at that time. It took her until 1946 to make any headway at all with the problem of identification, when she presented her paper 'Notes on some schizoid mechanisms', in which she described splitting processes and projective identification. Under the term 'projective identification' she described an omnipotent phantasy whereby, in combination with splitting processes, a part of the self can be split off and projected inside an object, and by that means take possession of its body, its mentality, and its identity. She described some of the consequences that arise from this confusion of identity: in particular claustrophobic anxieties and some of the severe persecutory anxieties related to claustrophobia.

The history of the so-called Kleinian group from 1946 on is by and large the history of the investigation of projective identification and splitting processes. The basic work done by Melanie Klein in the pregenital Oedipus complex and the technical development in child analysis are her original contributions. From 1946 on, the people who worked with her really got their teeth into this because it threw up a terrific snowstorm of phenomena and technical problems. It greatly widened the range of patients who could be approached through the psychoanalytic method. It gave them conceptual tools with which they could work in exploring phenomenology that they could not even notice previously.

The point about projective identification is that it is the description of a process by which a narcissistic identification comes about – that is, a process of the omnipotent phantasy of splitting off and projecting a part of the self into an external or internal object. This process results in phenomena of identification with the object of an immediate and somewhat delusional sort, which is the identification aspect of projective identification. Then it throws up a spectrum of phenomena related to the projection itself, which is related to the emotional and phantasy experiences of the part of the self that is inside, leading into claustrophobic anxieties and related things like hypochondria, depersonalisation states, confusion about time and space, and so on.

When I came on the scene in London in 1954, projective identification was used by the people in our group as synonymous with narcissistic identifications. We were comparing it with the processes of introjective identifications which Freud had described in relation to the genital Oedipus conflict and the establishment of the superego, and which Melanie Klein had moved to an earlier period in development by describing the introjection of the breast, both the good and bad breast, as part-objects. These internalised part-objects, preludes to the superego, she called superego or precursors of the superego. This process of introjective identification was being understood as something very different from a narcissistic identification in that it was not something that happened in a moment; an object was set up internally through introjection, and this object, primarily through its ego-ideal functions, would promulgate in the ego – or really in the self, as she would speak of it – a thrust for development along certain lines, an aspiration to become like the object, worthy of it: all of which was part of what she described as the depressive position.

At that time, we rather thought that the problem of narcissistic identifications was in a sense solved, conceptually speaking: that they were produced by projective identifications, and that was that. There was just the matter of exploring what began to look like an almost limitless field of phenomenology related to projective identification and its consequences. We got quite used to the term; it is not very poetic but it came easily off the tongue and we found ourselves saying 'projective identification… projective identification' in a quite blasé way. Of course we also began to notice that interpreting on the lines of projective identification did not seem to carry any weight in certain situations. We were in trouble with certain kinds of patients and saw that something else was going on that certainly was to do with identification processes. It was connected with narcissism but seemed to have a quite different phenomenology from that under the rubric of projective identification.

The first paper about it was finally produced by Esther Bick in 1988 as 'The function of the skin in early object relations'. There she described something in very early infantile development that she became aware of in her work with mothers and infants: something that had to do with catastrophic anxiety in certain infants whose mothers seemed somehow unable to contain them. When these infants became anxious their mothers became anxious too, and a spiral of anxiety tended to develop that ended with the infant going into a state of quivering – not a tantrum nor screaming but a disintegrated, disorganised state. Esther Bick began to observe this phenomenon also in certain patients, generally those who on the whole did not seem terribly ill: in candidates, in people who came because of problems such as poor work accomplishment, unsatis-factory social lives, vague pathological complaints; people on the periphery of the analytic community and wanted to have an analy-sis but could not quite say why. She began to observe that these patients in their dream life and in their waking life were subject to states of temporary disintegration very much like the infants. Suddenly they just would not be able to do anything. They would have to sit down, and they would shake. It was not that they were anxious in the ordinary sense of an anxiety attack; they just felt muddled, paralysed, and confused, and could not do anything. They just had to sit down or lie down until it went away. The material of the analysis at these times began to throw up images such as: a sack of potatoes getting wet and all the potatoes spilled out; or a patient suddenly wetting herself; or a patient's teeth falling out or his arms fell off, quite painlessly – material that described disintegration processes of some sort, something not held together, not contained.

Bick began to notice that these people all had disturbances related to the skin or their experience of the skin: not so much dermatological disorders as how they felt about the skin – that it was too thin, that it bruised easily, was easily lacerated, did not feel as if it had any strength to it, and so on. She discovered that this was a very pervasive kind of experience for these people, that they were not properly held together by a good skin, but had other ways of holding themselves together. In her paper on the skin, she describes some of these. Some held themselves together intellectually with their intelligent thinking and talking, the gift of the gab. They had explanations for everything and could hold themselves together with explanations. Bick felt she could observe situations in the disorganised infants showing that early verbalisations had been encouraged, and they became children who were prone to talking all the time, terrific chatterboxes. She observed in some adult patients that they seemed to hold them-selves together muscularly: they did callisthenics, weight-lifting, athletics, and their attitude towards life was a muscular one – that you did not think about a problem, you acted first and saw what happened and if that did not work out you did it another way, but you moved your muscles. Esther Bick discovered that she could trace similar processes in infants whose mothers encouraged them to be aggressive little boxers, to attack her with their fists, laughing in an excited way. It was a way of overcoming these states of anxiety or disintegration. She began to call these 'secondary skin formations', or 'substitute skin formations'.

All the time when she was describing this to me, back in the 1960s, she would hold her hands together and say 'they are sticky; they stick'. In analysis this felt like a patient who does not intend ever to finish the analysis: that they are on to something good and expect to be with you for the duration – plus six months. She also thought that these patients had some sort of difficulty about introjection and that they could not use projective identification very much – that their conception of their relationships was a very external one, their values very external and not generated by internal relations, not based on internal principles but on observation of themselves: their own reactions, but seen in the mirror of other people's eyes, copying, imitating, fashion-conscious, preoccupied with manners and social forms and social status. Not necessarily in an offensive way, or even in a way that one would have noticed. In fact, many of them were 'well-adjusted' – a hateful expression. They were well-adjusted people who would not ordinarily have come to analysis, had they not in most instances lived on the fringe of the analytic community where going into analysis was the thing to do. They most often came to analysis because some friend of theirs was in analysis.

Esther Bick had a vague feeling that there was something wrong with their identification processes: they did not use introjection very well; they did not learn from having experiences but merely by imitating other people. Of course our educational system is right up their alley, you might say, so they were often educationally very successful – rote learners, imitators, unimaginative.

At this time I was working with a group of child psychotherapists who were treating autistic children. I had worked with autistic children in the States, and I began supervising colleagues through the late 1950s and the 1960s: some eight or ten cases of autism being treated psychoanalytically drifted into supervision with me. We finally set up a little group and began to study and review the material. We began to discover things about autistic children that began to ring a bell: in some way, these discoveries were connected also with phenomena that Esther Bick was observing. Without going into the whole business of autistic children, I would like to emphasise a few of the major things that we discovered and that impressed us very much.

First of all, what impressed us about these children was that when we looked back after several years of psychoanalytic treatment of a child, we felt we could divide the phenomenology manifest in the consulting room into two categories. First, there was the category of purely autistic phenomena, which remained the same and never changed, consisting of an assortment of rather disparate items of behaviour with different objects in the room, and involving in a simple way particular senses and very simple activities. A child might always, on coming into a room, go and suck the latch on the window, or go to smell the plasticine, or go and lick the glass of the window – actions like that, very simple, very sensual. At first, of course, we had to assume that every item was meaningful and it must be related to every other item of behaviour: that all behaviour was strung together by a thread of meaning, and so on. These items did not change. They only shrank, as it were, from occupying nine-tenths of the session to begin with, to eventually occupying one-tenth of the session. They might even clear on Wednesday and only be present on Friday or Monday, before or after the weekend. Those seem to be the autistic items.

Then there was a second category of items that were more complicated; they were not repetitive. When you culled them out from the autistic matrix, you could string them together; and described to someone, they would sound like the ordinary play of a neurotic or psychotic child in the playroom, that could be examined psychoanalytically and sometimes even understood a bit. So we felt we were seeing in this matrix of autistic phenomena something very simple, very meaningless, very sensual, very repetitive, and in a sense a flight from mental life. In this sea of meaninglessness there were little items of meaningful experience that gradually began to agglutinate, to fill up the Wednesdays, fill up the middle of the week or the middle of the term. These children turned out to have incredible intolerance to separation. We did not at first think of these two categories in terms of dimensionality of life-space; we thought of them in terms of 'mental' and 'non-mental', as if in the autistic phenomena we were seeing something equivalent to what you might see in a *petit mal* seizure or in the automatism of the comatose patient.

It was only after we studied in retrospect children who had been in treatment for three, four, five years, what we began to think in terms of dimensionality and in terms of space and spatial relations – and with it, of course, the effect upon time relationships. What gradually emerged for us as we thought and talked about it was that outside the area of their autism, in what we came to think of as their post-autistic psychosis, these children functioned as if there really were no spaces – there were only surfaces, in two dimensions. Things were not solid: there were only surfaces they might lean up against, feel, smell, touch, or get some sensation from. They leaned up against surfaces, they leaned up against the analyst, they leaned up against the chest of drawers. They could not seem to crawl into places, as most children do. You would think they never had pockets – nothing ever went into their pockets. They did not seem to hold things well. Items just seemed to fall through them. They also gave the impression that they did not listen very well: you felt your words went right through them. Their responses often seemed so delayed that you felt all that had been left behind of what you said was a kind of musical disturbance that they eventually reacted to or reacted against. Their relationships to inside and outside the playroom were very characteristic in that they seemed not really to distinguish between being inside and being outside. With one little boy it was quite typical that when he came into the playroom, he would rush to the window to see if there were any birds in the garden; and at first, if he saw any birds, he would be terrifically triumphant. We assumed this meant that he was inside and they were outside. But then in a moment it changed, and he felt very persecuted and began shaking his fist at them, and then he would run over to the analyst and look into his mouth or into his ears, and it seemed fairly clear that a reversal had taken place. From being inside and the birds outside, it had suddenly reversed, and he was outside and they were inside – inside the analyst, inside the building, undistinguished by him. Another child tended to draw pictures of houses, one on each side of the paper; and when you held it up to the light, you saw that the doors were superimposed – a kind of house where you open the front door and step out of the back door at the same time.

We came to understand that these children were having difficulty in conceptualising or experiencing a space that could be closed. In a space that cannot be closed, there is no space at all. Then we had the exciting experience of seeing some of them begin to close these orifices. One boy, for instance, went through a period in which he papered the walls of the playroom and papered the walls of his room at home; then he began to draw pictures of maps, and these maps consisted mainly of the route between his home and the consulting-room. At first these pictures seemed to be of terrible things happening – absolute chaos and disorder: one minute, police cars that seemed to turn into criminals, the next, soldiers turning into madmen, and so on. Gradually, over a period of months, stop-lights and little Royal Canadian mounted policemen began to appear in these drawings, and slowly order seemed to settle. Then he began to draw pictures of the inside of the clinic where he was being seen. There began to be rooms, doors; rooms began to have separate functions. These pictures were very exciting, because they all looked like the insides of bodies. They did not look like the insides of buildings at all. These children could take an object that was so open that getting inside it was impossible because you fell out and the inside was like a house without a roof; it rained inside as well as out, so you might as well stay out. Then they gradually began to close the orifices of their objects to make a space, and development – particularly language development – began to take place.

It was at that time that we began to think about dimensionality and the autistic phenomena proper as a kind of mindlessness in which there was only a tropism relationship, with one direction. For instance, a child would come in and run right up to the window and suck on the latch or run between two doors – one door which he smelled and the other which he locked.

Then there was the two-dimensional surface relationship to objects in which there were no spaces and in which, therefore, identification processes could not take place. It seemed development could not occur because they could use neither projective identification – which required a space to get into – nor introjective identification, which required a space that you could take something into. We did notice that these children had another kind of identification – that we felt we could really call imitation. One could see it sometimes in their posture, sometimes in their tone of voice. Suddenly from a little mite of a boy a deep voice would come out saying 'bad boy'. One could notice it in relation to their clothing: they would insist on items that were the same colour as the analyst had worn the day before. One could see how difficult it was for them to take an interest in anything new: it was always the thing that had interested and attracted the attention of the analyst that would be repeated over and over again.

We began to see a link between the autistic children and Esther Bick's observations with her patients and the infants. We began to think we were now observing a new kind of narcissistic identification, and that we could no longer think of projective identification as being synonymous with narcissistic identification. Narcissistic identification was the broader term, with projective identification subsumed under it, as defence had become a broader term with repression subsumed under it. We decided to call this new form of narcissistic identification *adhesive identification*. It involved a process closely connected with mimicry and with the shallowness and externalisation of values that Esther Bick observed in the patients I described to you.

Time, as in four-dimensionality, was not implied. In fact, a proper relation to time is a very sophisticated achievement. We began to observe that the two-dimensional patients had a very oscillating relationship to time: that it went in one direction, then back, and then another and came back, but did not really move. When they came out of this oscillation and became more three-dimensional, concerned with spaces, they had a more circular and cyclical relationship with time: day and night were different but always came back to the same spot; time did not get anywhere, and you did not really grow older. Something grew bigger, something shrivelled up and died, but you did not get older in any inevitable way. Ageing was a kind of accident due to poor planning, or negligence, or the aggression of other people.

The progression to four-dimensionality, to an appreciation of time as a linear process and to a lifetime as a thing with a definable beginning and end came much later. Little Hans thought that he had always been in the stork box before he came out. That was a fairly sophisticated idea and had something to do with the achievement of what Melanie Klein had described as the depressive position – that is, a shift from egocentricity and preoccupation with one's own self, safety, and comfort, to a primary concern with the welfare of one's objects. These processes connected with confusion about time, and attitudes towards time could now be noticed more in the phenomenology of the consulting-room and brought into the interpretive work.

So we coined the term 'adhesive identification', and the more we thought about it, the more we began to notice that it played a part in much of our patients' lives and in our own lives. This was particularly true in relation to values: the difficulty in establishing internal values, that is, an internal source of values. For instance, one noticed in people who were artistic and seemed to have good taste in art and be very knowledgeable about it, that they often reported that they knew very well there was something wrong because when they went to a gallery, they always looked at the title and the name of the artist before looking at the picture. They wanted to know its value before actually looking at it. This was, in a sense, a prototype of their attitude towards the world. They wanted to know the price of things because they had no basis internally for establishing their own personal evaluation of it in terms of its meaningfulness to them. We discovered patches of shallowness present in everybody, patches in which emotionality was very attenuated – not a sense of flatness, but of thinness, a kind of squeakiness of emotional response.

We think that in our own way of working we are beginning to open up a new area of phenomenology; we have a conceptual tool with which we can pry things open and begin to see phenomena that we had not noticed before. Where it will lead and how it will enrich our work is a bit too soon to tell.

Addendum²

Now this was all about the time that Dr Bion's series of books was coming out; *Learning from Experience* had already come out and had influenced us greatly. *The Elements of Psychoanalysis* had come out and knocked us all down, as it were, and it took us years to begin to grasp what in the world he was talking about. *Transformations* was even more traumatic. I must say, it has taken me many years to discover the tremendous impact those books had on me. It was really only when I undertook to teach a course at the Tavistock Clinic on Dr Bion's work and was absolutely forced to transform what I thought I understood about it into actual knowledge about what I understood about it and to put it into words for other people that I began to grasp what a tremendous influence it had had on my thinking. And, of course, what is central to Dr Bion's ideas are these concepts of container and contained which link so much to our work with autistic children and to Mrs Bick's work. And then, of course, Bion's incredible step forward into a real theory of thinking for the first time, I think, in psychoanalysis: the theory of alpha-function and the Grid.

...

I don't think that adhesive identifications or introjective iden-tifications have anything to do with swallowing. I think that introjective identification is something that comes about in a most mysterious way through an intensely cooperative relationship between an object that wishes to project and an object that wishes to accept the projection. It's not only the baby that introjects from the breast, it's also the mother who introjects the baby. Not simply accepts the projection of distressed parts of the self as Dr Bion has described in order to return them to the baby in a less distressed state. But the mother does also introject the baby as a person in her internal world and the baby introjects from the mother not simply a breast or nipple and not simply a mother, but introjects what the mother wishes to project into the baby which generally we assume is a mother and father, a united couple, a combined object. So it isn't much related to swallowing and different kinds of swallowing or cannibalistic internalisations, as it used to be called. It seems

---

2 Extracts from a talk at the Psychoanalytic Center of California, 1979, transcribed by Jennifer Langham.

to me that introjection is a much more mysterious mind-to-mind process which may go on and perhaps optimally does go on in the infant-breast relationship; that is, the infant-mother relationship at the moment when the mother is feeding the infant with the breast--the baby is getting its nourishment from the breast. The introjective processes are mind-to-mind processes.

...

In talking about two-dimensionality, it's true that, as in the patient described by Mrs Bick, that it is very common in patients who have a leaky containment. The point about two-dimensionality is that it relates to the object quite outside the sphere of containment. Two-dimensionality can function as a defensive position, you might say, rather than as a specific defence against anxiety. It is equivalent to what in war communiqués used to be called 'withdrawing to a more strategic position'. That's not the same as defending yourself against the enemy. It's a euphemism for retreating, and I certainly have seen two-dimensionality to be a position to which people retreat at a moment when they are threatened with panicky affect. That doesn't make it a mechanism of defence.

Dismantling is quite a different thing. In the autism book, I tried to relate it to certain aspects of fetishism and to the so-called transitional objects and to certain aspects of obsessionality in general. This is a dismantling of the sensory apparatus insofar as it is, most of the time, automatically treated in what Dr Bion calls a common sense way, or what Harry Stack Sullivan called 'consensuality'. Dismantling is the dismantling of that consensuality into discrete sensory modes of perception and relationship to the world, and it's something quite different from two-dimensionality as we were seeing it and describing it.

We thought in the autistic children that dismantling was very clearly a flight from overwhelming depressive anxiety impinging on an as-yet extremely primitive personality structure. I would say it was a flight rather than a defence. You see, one of the things that you have to consider is the problem of the sense of identity, so that what presents itself to you in the consulting room at any moment is really that part of the personality that is, you might say, in possession of the organ of consciousness; that organ for the perception of psychic qualities, the possession of which carries with it a sense of identity. That I, at that particular moment, am that part of myself that is in possession of my organ of consciousness.

Now, what happens, which you see most obtrusively in adolescence, is that different parts of the self which are split from one another come into possession of that organ of consciousness from moment to moment, day to day; it's as if you are talking to a different person who hardly remembers what happened yesterday. Well, the same thing happens in many flights from pain that don't really constitute a regression in the sense of a loss of organization of the structure of the personality; that more primitive parts of the personality are allowed to take over this organ of consciousness and the sense of identity and to use their particular modes of relating to the world and to relate to the world that they experience.

A patient may shift from three- to two-dimensionality, from four- to three- to two-dimensionality, by shifting the contact that you're making in the transference with different parts of the personality without any regression taking place at all. And therefore, it isn't really correct, I think, in terms of theory, to call it either regression or a mechanism of defence. It is really a shift of the point of contact with the personality – that is, the point of contact offered to the world at that particular moment.

One can sometimes see adhesive identification, projective identification, and introjective identification operating in sequence in a single patient. I heard in a supervision today about a patient who at first was quite clearly presenting two dimensional material and then suddenly shifted over into three dimensional material about the babies inside the mother. It ended up with a yearning for a good father that he could identify with, who would refurbish this mother and bring her babies back to life so he wouldn't have to be out on the snowy slope. I mean, I absolutely saw the material shift from two to three dimensionality to introjective identification. And I would think that good sessions often can be traced in quite a different way from the sort of sequence that I demonstrated in *The Psychoanalytical Process* which was really a cycle of object relationships at a three dimensional and possibly four dimensional level. With patients who have two dimensional tendencies, you can see within a single session the cycle of dimensionality.

CHAPTER SIXTEEN

'Patches of blue': the decline of the male[1]

(1998)

I should say something about being invited to be keynote speaker at a seminar like this, because I myself haven't got anywhere close to the millennium yet. My point of view comes from a sort of Victorian folly called psychoanalysis, which is still struggling out of the 19th century as far as I can see, and has an extremely limited view of the culture we live in, derived second-hand from our parents. This is only slightly augmented by the fact that I have travelled very widely, teaching in various places, and that gives me a view of other cultures. Also, I come from a different culture myself, and that makes the culture of this country very vivid to me by contrast. When I came here in 1954 the contrast was very great, but, thanks to the vulgarisation of the Thatcher era, it is no longer so great. Very disappointing, but there it is. It's largely the consequences of this vulgarisation that I am (probably) going to talk about. It seems to me that the bombardment by the entertainment industry, the alteration in values of the Thatcher era in favour of wealth production and so on, the scramble for social status

---

1 Talk given in 1998, with thanks to Dorothy Hamilton.

promoted by the car industry, has had a tremendous effect on the male population, starting very early. It has seduced boys back to the television and later their computer games, and to the sort of secret culture that is fairly unknown to their parents' generation; this has given them a sense of superiority over their parents and has emboldened them, you might say, in relation to parental values and parental expectations.

The impact on the girl population has been quite different. It seems to have accelerated puberty by at least two years, both physical and mental, and has, it seems to me, had also an emboldening [empowering] effect on them, but in a very different way that strikes one as being both useful and probably rather admirable. You might say they are no longer frightened of being raped. Well, bravo. So they walk home alone at night and often get assaulted in one way or another, but it doesn't seem to be the devastating experience their mothers might have expected. It is in line with being whistled at by the workmen in the street, which they are very blasé about.

So we have this fundamental divergence between the sexes, with the boys becoming more withdrawn, more passive, more gregarious in a pub sort of way, and failing to develop interests at school. They don't necessarily do badly at school, but they certainly lack interest, and do not develop passions for anything except their Nintendo games or those peculiar skates that they spring around on. Their passionate life seems to me markedly withdrawn and markedly skewed in the direction of passivity, and, when asked for a title, I gave 'The decline of the male' because I think this is something that is happening, and is worrying individually but also worrying in terms of the culture. I see the difference on the faces of the young people as I drive along the High Street in Oxford on the way to work. The boys look really dishevelled, rather dispirited in their facial expressions, a bit weak in their eyes; and the girls stride along in a manner that used to be called manful. And what I hear from my undergraduate patients seems to bear out this alteration: that the girls have to seek out the boys, which amounts to a kind of sharing of the television culture and leads directly into mutual masturbation, homosexuality and so on. The boys expect to be sought out and, if they are at all good-looking, seem tremendously to fancy themselves as irresistible; the struggle with them in analysis is to get them to be interested in anything. They seem to be pure examples of Freud's pleasure principle, and words like 'easy' and 'fun' and 'holiday' sprinkle their vocabularies in a way that squeezes out anything like 'love' and 'adventure', 'excitement' and 'desire' and so on.

The transition that one expects psychoanalytically from puberty to adolescence and from adolescence to the beginnings of adulthood seems very blurred. The boys' gang and the girls' gang of puberty seems to carry on – at least for the boys, not so much for the girls – and the transition from adolescent boyhood to manhood is very retarded for the boys, so that they remain boyish almost indefinitely. They are usually jogged out of it to some extent by the birth of their first child, but somehow they often do not emotionally engage in that experience of life, of reproduction. It seems to impinge on them primarily as a deprivation – deprivation of sleep, deprivation of sex, deprivation of attention from their partners or wives or concubines of whoever they happen to have produced the child by – because they are busy, it seems to me, with the only thing that interests them deeply and that is status; and status is equated with money and earnings, and the kind of car you drive and the kind of holidays you take.

I sympathise with them in a way in their loss of athletic interests in favour of body-building – which seems to be mainly a narcissistic pursuit – because the sports that interest them are ones that are tremendously commercialised and invite spectator participation, such as football. But even the more individual sports have been a bit spoiled by the invention of superior equipment – the marvellous tennis racket which enables anybody to play tennis, the marvellous ski boot that enables anybody to ski – and I think this takes a lot of the pleasure out of accomplishment in these sports. What they get left with is golf, which remains challenging because, no matter how good the clubs and the balls, playing golf is really an art that very few people master, and certainly hardly anybody masters without lessons. So I do notice that the men become very obsessed with golf, to a degree that drives their wives to distraction; that they disappear at weekends, and they disappear mentally too, because they are mentally searching for balls in the rough, missing putts, and wondering how Tiger Woods does it. It is amazing the excellence with which golf is played professionally and, of course, also the vast sums that are earned these days which seem, for the male, to carry on the momentum of the Thatcher era.

The transition on the other hand of the women, from girlhood to womanhood, seems to me to be both social and much more biological, in spite of the ads we are confronted with telling us that size makes a big difference and being 'bigger than John's' and so on. The girls seem fairly quickly to get over being impressed by the male organ and its capacity for erection, and the idea of babies does take hold of them very powerfully. Culturally speaking, they seem to be confronted with a situation where they expect disappointment, and you hear and see things about how to get rid of your husband but keep the children, as a kind of aim in life: how to be a single parent family, how to fight your ex-husband in the courts. The idea of the meeting of the sexes in a happy co-operative adventure seems to survive in a sort of minimal group who have been fortunate enough to have the kind of parents who were really united, and with whom we find analytically that the unconscious concept of a combined object is really in them.

Whereas it does seem to be absent in most adult males and females who seem to have carried over the blatant superior separation and incommunicado status of their objects, and their therefore unresolved Oedipal conflicts, so that, when the women become ravished by their desire for children, they are at a bit of a loss from the point of view of identification processes, and many of them opt for negative identifications – that is, finding fault with their mothers and trying to do the opposite. Within five to ten years they discover they are doing exactly the same: they are screaming at their children, threatening them, depriving them of contact and so on – where their intention had been to do exactly the opposite.

Now as I say, this is really a view from this peculiar folly of the analytic consulting room and it is in a sense an old man's view as well. It is bound to say 'we did better and we had it better, and I don't know what is happening to the younger generation'. But, invited to a meeting like this, I'm bound to say what I think, though it's not very encouraging. But I think the encouraging thing is that this very biological passion that women have for babies is overcoming what I called, in my little introduction, the male biblical fear of the woman. I think that male dominance and male bullying and tyranny has always been based on fear of the woman, and very fundamentally on fear of her genitalia, those bleeding, unclean genitalia of the biblical days, the powerful seductive genitalia of Tamar and Ruth [Delilah, Jezebel] – irresistible. The fear of the female genitals has been overcome to a certain extent in men and boys by improved anatomical knowledge, but I'm afraid anatomical knowledge is not much more use in these matters than knowing the names of parts of your car when it breaks down. Noise in the carburettor – what does that mean? It creates a sense of knowledge and mastery, but in fact the female is more mysterious today than she was apprehended to be in the past, when she was frighteningly unclean and her belly was getting swollen periodically, and she was turning all her passion and feelings towards this child.

Today her mentality is much more mysterious to men, and it seems to me it's a very difficult thing for them to pay attention to. They tend, instead of paying attention to the mystery of their woman's mentality, to be content to try to attract her attention and her interest in *their* mentality – which unfortunately tends, with the help of the advertising media, to mean attention and interest in their genitals. I think they are losing that game, that the women are beginning to realise something about the anatomy also – to realise that the penis is just a conduit through which the semen and the urine flows, and it is not an organ of remarkable interest any more than it is an organ of remarkable beauty, so that the male population is losing its pulling power, you might say, its attraction. It's true that the male body is very beautiful when it is in good condition and when it is employed in a graceful and effective way, but it takes a great deal of love for a woman to see the male genitals as beautiful. The pubertal and pre-pubertal girl may be in awe of them because there is a lot of fear of them, but once the fear is overcome, they then lost their fascination and the power of dominion.

But there is a great mystery in the female internal genitals, with their production of eggs, insemination and fertilisation and the growth of the foetus. The beauty of this mystery, it seems to me, lies behind the enhanced self-respect that one finds in women. It doesn't have much to do with gaining the vote or having access to employment and income. I think it has a lot to do with the recognition of the mystery of the beauty of the reproductive process, in relation which, of course the male – although his function in producing semen is equally mysterious, but can be so degraded by semen banks and such things, which are equivalent really to keeping the men as studs – the male reproductive capacity has lost its kudos, because it has lost its beauty for the imagination. I don't think this is irrecoverable, but it is in dire straits at the moment, it seems to me. It is worth remembering that Freud's whole theory of castration anxiety never mentioned the testicles, was all penis, and somehow male psychology hasn't much caught up with this problem. It is not so true in the Mediterranean and South American cultures, where a man is spoken of with admiration as having big balls. Well, that's hopeful.

Now, the victim in this has been the process called falling in love, and the differentiation between making love and having sex. The term 'making love' is used either with embarrassment, or in such an automatic tick-like way as to be meaningless, so that people seem largely to mean having sex or, in fact, masturbating one another. The cult of the orgasm is linked to the cult of the erect penis. 'Good in bed' seems to mean giving orgasms because of the size of the penis and the vigour with which it is accomplished. I think it's a sad story but I think it is fairly clear that the dawn, the renaissance that is coming is a renaissance connected with the beauty and mystery of the reproductive process.

One of the troubles about it is that, at the present time, by the time children reach puberty and adolescence, most of them inflict such distress on their parents that it is very hard for parents to look forward to their growing up; but that does seem to me to be cultural and it is not universal. It is certainly connected with things like the rate of unemployment and the loss of job security, all of which, along with the destruction of the Labour Unions, were the main accomplishments of the Thatcher era, which ushered in this craze for privatisation. The disillusionment with these processes is accumulating. I notice, for instance, that the differentiation between Communism and Stalinism has finally penetrated fairly widely, and I am interested to see that a Communist has been asked to form the new government in Italy – but of course the Communist party in Italy never was Stalinist as far as I know.

So I don't want to convey to you the idea that I am gloomy about the future because I have to die so the rest can go to hell. I really do feel very optimistic, but my optimism is rooted first of all in the women, and their filling the vacuum of vitality left by this withdrawal of the male population from their own imagination, interest and passion. But as always, my trust is in the artistic community, that is not going to be swallowed up by the commercialisation of art, and by the media and the film industry and the entertainment industry, but is going to state its ideas and its attitudes and feelings artistically. It is probably music that will pull us through eventually. It is a great shame that much less music is taught in schools, both primary and secondary, and parents seem to be less and less willing to spend the time and money to get their children taught an instrument. And of course, if you can play the television and Nintendo games, who wants to blow a flute? But I think eventually even the terrible pop music begins to sound a bit musical, and they will eventually learn that they do have good instruments and the instruments will teach them. I am a bit more worried about the artists, because of the modern things like acrylics replacing oil-painting, and the brush and the spray-gun replacing technique; but we have museums full of old masters, and I am heartened to see that the museums are more and more crowded. The galleries that sell modern works are not crowded.

What I am trying to convey to you from this really severely behind-the-times point of view is that, seen from the vantage point of say, 1950, things look terrible. One is always nostalgically distorting the past, but still there has been a marked change in values, and with it a marked change in culture. I am trying to see what Richard in Mrs Klein's *Narrative of a Child Analysis* called 'patches of blue'.

The architectonics of paranoia[1]

(1999)

The topic of paranoia constitutes an addendum to the Claustrum, in that it has to do with projective identification and pseudomaturity; these are the highroad to paranoia.

Paranoia, from the structural point of view, is a kind of Gothic edifice, ugly and useless, but durable beyond all expectation. Of course in this analogy (not a metaphor) the enigma of the durability resides in the secret perpetual maintenance. Consequently the lauded art treasure of the cathedral is always frustratingly hidden behind the scaffolding and workmen's sheets, drapes, etc. I am not going to report on any particular paranoid patient but rather an assembly of traits common to this disorder.

The engineering of a Gothic cathedral, to follow the analogy, is hopelessly inefficient, resting a greatly expanded roof on massive walls supported by crude buttressing. Inside this massive and inefficient exterior we find an interior of surprising delicacy and beauty in the vaulting, arches and window tracery. The paradox of massive exterior, derived from a Roman

---

1 Talk given in 1999.

fortress, to a delicate interior shows that there was no dearth of the engineering skill but something more sinister at work. History shows the Roman vulgarising of Greek architecture and statuary in favour of likeness, with Emperors becoming Gods, favouring 'reality' in art. Fascism did the same two millennia later, sacrificing beauty to likeness, just as it sacrificed humanist values to heavy-handed justice.

The character of the paranoiac presents to the analyst similarly a defiant grandiosity buttressed by pessimism which, like the cathedral walls are composed of durable material called 'facts' inside which airy structures called 'the history' of the patient's development can be built, strung together by beautiful theories unconcerned about authenticity. Like the limestone building blocks with their fossils of pre-terrestrial life forms, a certain authenticity is given to confabulated history, disregarding the translation from the bottom (of the sea) to the head (mountain tops) thanks to seismic disturbance. When the facts of observation are said to contain the meaning as self-evident, a road is opened to persuasive propaganda based on the failure to distinguish between memory and recall. The secret of this persuasive and even intimidating recall lies in what Woody Allen calls the secret of his being such a skilled lover, namely practice in solitude.

Similarly the verbatim recall of events by the paranoiac rests upon his immediate transformation of the event into a news-story, the words of which can be recalled and do not have to be reconstructed as in a memory, full of approximation.

This transformation of observation into words which are said to contain the meaning, omits the musical component of communication. Faced with this verbal, litigious recall, the analyst, who of course cannot pretend to remember with his approximate reconstruction, is reduced to saying that the patient's recall does not sound like the analyst's language but like the patient's. This is a weak defence but as an invitation to dialogue it can be effective.

This sense of certainty, built upon a sense of omniscience depending on confabulation and recall, constructs a wall of omniscience which seems impenetrable, and from behind which the paranoiac can only be smoked out by evoking the claustrophobia incipient in it.

Like the Gothic cathedral the ugliness of the paranoiac's state of mind strikes one in its towers and spires. He knows what is wrong with the world and what needs to be done. Of course it always turns out to be a final solution like the wisdom of Solomon, that the baby must be cut in half, the heart of compromise and egalitarianism. This final solution by splitting and projective identification rids the self of unwanted parts by anal expulsion, which results in the sense of the nest being fouled by the new babies, the arse-hole view of a polluted and dying planet.

By virtue of this pessimistic world-view, the paranoiac is always close to suicide, which is his 'last resort' in the battle with his persecutors. This points the way to the therapy of paranoia, namely the evoking of the latent despair due to emergence of claustrophobia which comes through as the world is seen in projective states when the grandiosity is dismantled. Of course the edge of the cliff of suicide tries the courage of the analyst.

By means of the analogy to the structure of the Gothic cathedral, I would hope to bring into view the contrast between a political or corporate view of the world and that based on individuality, what Bion has called the 'work group', characterised by individual passionate interest, Socratic justice through 'minding your own business', and quiet work away from the limelight. This powerful quietness, free of grandiosity, aware of the unconscious nature of wisdom with its dependence on internal objects, produces the humility which gives access to the aesthetic level of thought and perhaps eventually even to a spiritual level.

This description of the plight of the paranoiac does not take into account the balance of pleasure and pain which can be worked out through this verbal facility and the power of confabulated recall. The political potentialities are considerable and evoke cult-formation often of a dangerous and satanic sort. But even the success of becoming the leader of a cult does not significantly alter the paranoiac's sense of being outside the human race, the pariah, the orphan, deprived of brothers and sisters. Resources of contempt for the complacency, bourgeois values, rigidity and impoverishment of family life and values cannot protect the paranoiac from pressing his nose to the world from which he feels excluded. Its explosiveness in the transference is the entrée to the world or rather the egress from the claustrum. Despite all the confabulatory arguments and achievements of being the star of the show the paranoiac cannot escape from the insincerity of his voice, the voice that is always pretending to pretend to pretend. Words without music are meaningless, logic without experience is empty.

Finally a word needs to be added regarding the strongly split bisexuality of the paranoiac, which has not only led analysts to assume the disorder's basis in homosexuality but torments the paranoiac himself with doubts. It does seem evident in analytic investigation that the balance in the gender experience is very delicate, with strong aggressive and muscular emotions in the female and strong passivity and yearnings to be cosseted in the male. While certainly implying lack of femininity or masculinity, it does not imply any very positive inversion or perversion of sexual desires. On the contrary the yearnings for a reciprocal intimacy tend to be very weak and are replaced by the sense of grievance, often toward nature, cosmic injustice which spurs on a thirst for revenge against the human race.

But characteristically the suffering in the paranoiac lends itself to a resolution through projection of the sense of being betrayed by life, that is to become a betrayer, the mark of the psychopathic personality. This is a vast area that needs separate development.

Clinical examples[2]

Every once in a while one runs into a combination of patients who are exhibiting such similar behaviour that it's very instructive. I have had for a number of years three patients who are great talkers – in the sense of great arguers: born lawyers. Between the three of them they make my life a bit miserable. They insist that I like it. One of them who spent years in the army says I'm a born soldier, I like fighting. They do seem to me to have been children for whom family life ceased to exist once they started talking. They established a pseudomaturity on the basis of their gifted use of language – through the discovery of the ambiguity of language, of words. And what characterises them is the loss of music in their voice. Now of course this is true of obsessionality

---

2 This section is taken from a talk for the GERPEN, Paris, in 2000, published in French in *Meltzer à Paris*.

in general; and these patients are at the extreme of obsessionality in the sense of really being borderline psychotic. The borderline quality consists in their loss of any method for testing reality. The testing of reality by what Bion calls 'common sense' is replaced by a litigious belief in the concreteness of language, particularly any language that is in print. It is known to my patients that I have been 'in print' and this convinces them that I am a member of their guild – that I must believe in what I say. I explain that I have completely abandoned believing anything: that in my mind, believing is closely connected with having secrets, which is the infantile idea which children use to hide themselves inside their heads from the adults.

The 'secrets' of these patients vary. With one young woman in her very early thirties it is very concretely expressed in terms of 'I don't know anything about her because she never tells me her secrets', to which I say I'm not in the slightest interested in her secrets, because I don't believe in these children's ways of hiding themselves from their parents. As far as I'm concerned the truth about her is *revealed* in her behaviour; and her behaviour is that of a child brought up on the streets. She is a very pretty child and looks about thirteen, but she is as hard as nails. She is so unbearable I haven't begun to like her yet. Her language quickly reverts to obscenity, abuse, and contempt. Her ability to learn is absolutely minimal, although she is an expert at mimicry and has of course managed to get herself what looks like an education, with a university degree at Oxford; but she shows absolutely no evidence of having imbibed any culture. Of course Oxford is full of examination-passers, full of pseudomature children who have been propelled through Oxford like guided missiles, bathed in a sense of elitism, then fall into a panic when they graduate and don't know what to do because nothing interests them.

Now that dearth of interest is really what characterises this whole group. Instead of interest they are great gatherers of infor-mation. This information-gathering depends on the function of recall. Now recall is not the same as memory; memory is a reconstructive process; recall is an automatic process very much like a computer. It is of course a very intimidating capability, this recall of facts and information. It is the armament of every politi-cian, and is the reason why training in the law is so popular with politicians. It all has the structure of litigiousness: argument on the basis of information, accompanied by an assertion of logic. The logic that is involved utilizes certain favourite phrases like 'inevitable' and 'therefore' and '*QED*', the language of mathematics and particularly of geometry, and it is very difficult to demonstrate to these patients the lack of music in their voice and therefore the lack of meaning.

Now this reliance on recall gives rise to a certain type of relationship to the world in which what would ordinarily constitute observation and produce the evidence on which memories are constructed is replaced by a very strange process of confabulation. Patients like this constantly read back to you things you said yesterday, last month, last year, the first time they ever came to the consulting room – word for word. The only thing you can say is it doesn't sound like *your language*. But the patient, like the little lawyers that they are, insist their court record is 'word perfect'. Of course that is one of the computer languages – 'Word Perfect'.

The paranoia to which this leads is built on these confabulations. And they generally reach back into infancy. Patients like this give you a history that reaches back to the day they were born. One patient was born 'with a crooked back', and would creep into my consulting room as if she were 80 years old. Another patient's history goes back to her mother having an affair at the time she was born; the evidence for this is that her parents divorced and her mother remarried, but the rest is assumption. The important thing is that we are dealing with projective identification – of a kind that I have previously reported piecemeal and couldn't put together until very recently; one of them was the paper on 'delusion of clarity of insight' [see *The Claustrum,* 1992]. The picture of the world constructed from these confabulations is (like my street-girl) a world where every man is for himself. There is no concept of the family as a type of organisation that is different from 'every man for survival'. The idea that such a picture actually corresponds to the real world is very cogent if you move outside the family structure. If the newspapers told us about the *whole* world, that's the kind of world it would be: everything from fraud to genocide. With such a worldview, the idea that everything is permissible in the name of survival seems very reasonable: it's life in the jungle, even if it's the asphalt jungle – it is very *reasonable.*

And these views of history, of sociology, of politics, are the roots of paranoia.

Now family structure (which the newspapers thinks is *passé*) is something which has developed only gradually since the last Ice Age. The history of religion which has been so male-dominated shows us why: either God was a brute, or the gods were promiscuous adolescents – take your choice. Under these types of aegis it is not surprising that family structure developed very slowly, and things like aristocracy, primogeniture, and waiting for daddy to die to inherit his estate, were the basis of everyday life. The note of hope in *Lysistrata* didn't come to anything; women did not seize their power and exercise it. Today when they feel their power, they are split by it, into those who would promote the 'couple family' [3] and those who would keep a few males as stud as it were.

As I say the world of paranoia is the world of the newspapers and is taken as reality. And historically it is the world of reality. But not everyone's. And this is the stand one has to take with these lawyers and their assertions that everything is justified by survival. They are great statisticians and are ready to think up statistics at a moment's notice. Their favourite statistic is 'everybody' – that means, everybody is like themselves. Then what are you doing here in my consulting room? The answer is, they have come to teach you, to redeem you from your errors, to enlist you for their personal religion of survival.

The treatment of paranoia from my own experience is seldom successful. Any improvement can only be traced in qualitative terms. Something gradually softens. One patient, whom I am beginning to like, characteristically comes into the session like a lion and leaves like a lamb. But the lamb is only in the last five minutes, when she weeps and hopes that I won't die tomorrow, and asserts that I'm her only hope. But the first 45 minutes she chews me up and ridicules me, telling me I am wasting my time because she has been like this since the day she was born – and it may be true that she was one of these babies who (like an autistic child whom I supervise) bites the breast. Her descriptions are of

3 This phrase ('couple family') is missing in the tape in both English and French; it is inserted in view of the categories given in the 'child-in-the-family-in-the-community' as presented in *The Educational Role of the Family* (Harris Meltzer Trust, 2013).

a psychotic mother. I tell her I don't believe it; her parents lived together for 40 years; they bore and raised two children, herself and her hated sister; and I don't really believe that she is self-made and taught herself from books. I do tend to believe that she joined the army because she hoped to kill someone. And I'm almost ready to believe that she is intent on killing me eventually.

This is my idea of the nature of paranoia: that it is built on the basis of a projective identification with the mother's head-breast, with the use of mother's eyes and a perception of their omniscience – eyes which don't see evidence but 'facts'; and from this seeing of 'facts' they confabulate a picture of the world that suits them. The word 'know' is seldom out of their mouths. Such patients are constantly referring to what they are trying to show you, teach you, help you to understand. Along with their pessimistic view of the world, which justifies their philosophy of life-by-survival, is essentially a theory of taking over the world by killing everybody else. This military patient of mine is told by *her* patients that she is the most hated woman in Oxford; it is a point of pride since the most hated is equivalent to being the most famous.

Central to all this is the idea of intelligence. There is a great belief in the maldistribution of intelligence. Therefore a belief in 'genius', not as creativity but as speed of mental activity, and of course the speed at which their minds work is quite daunting. You are constantly having to ask them to slow down so that you have time to think about things, which of course is the basis for their patronising you – 'poor Dr Meltzer, he's getting old'. They will not understand that the musical faculty is the basis of thinking, because this is where the meaning of words is hidden.

When you reach the point in the therapy of these patients when they begin to hear how flat and unmusical their voice is, they try very hard to imitate a musical voice. But unconvincingly. It's as unconvincing as a child who sits at the piano and pretends to play it. I can easily believe that that child can hear music; but nobody else will hear music. Imitation is their answer to the whole mystery of introjection, and reveals how this belief that language is made up of words (as if words weren't equivocal) leads directly to two-dimensionality, and this two-dimensionality is easily decorated to be paranoia. The gradual softening of the paranoia comes from the gradual softening of the words. I think the technique for softening the words is to constantly request the patient to tell you the *meaning* of their words. Of course at first this is taken to be that you are asking for synonyms; it takes a long time for them to understand that you are interested in the musical *key* in which the word is being *sung*. So one puts one's faith in this softening process, that eventually talking will turn into singing, and words will cease to be used as armaments, implements of attack, and will begin to be sung as instruments of communication, with great relief to all around, both the patient and the therapist. So with the patient who is a lamb for the last five minutes of the session, it is possible to look forward to it, which enables you to sit through the 45 minutes of attack and assault with some degree of calm and comfort; and wait for the five minutes to become ten minutes, and eventually twenty minutes, and so on.

In all of this, one theme is that when the mind is cut off from the body, the body doesn't cease its participation in mental life, but automatically transforms emotional experiences into psychosomatic ones; indicating that there is no use trying to analyse psychosomatic symptoms. One pays attention to the world that the patient is living in, knowing very well that when they do manage to join the human race, their psychosomatic symptoms will just melt away. This military lady who used to creep into my consulting room complaining that the whole place smelled from the drains, can walk from her car with a certain swing; her whole personality takes on a bit of colour and jauntiness. So long as she doesn't cough before her head hits the pillow, we may hear a dream instead of a litany of paranoid complaints about her work.

Always, the dream is the instrument by which the world of richness and symbol formation is contacted. So there is a crucial moment at the beginning of the session when either the patient coughs (and you're in for it) or tells you a dream and you have some interesting work to do. The first and last sessions of the week tend to be a dead loss apart from the last five minutes, but the middle session is a haven. So one of the technical challenges of such patients is that you learn how to defend yourself against these accusations of what you said yesterday and the week or year before. 'Those don't *sound* like my words' – that's all you can say. Whereupon you are treated as senile so it doesn't matter.

Work, play, and sublimation[1]

(1973)

Since adult sexuality is guided by introjective identification, it seems paradoxical, chicken-and-egg style, to relate the terms 'work' and 'sexuality' to one another in adult life. To take work as the wider term and subsume sexuality as a particular area of work would seem common sense, from a descriptive point of view. Nonetheless, in the realm of the meaning of behaviour as investigated by the psychoanalytical method, the term 'sexual' appears to be the wider of the two, especially when its 'parental' quality is recognised. Adult play would then have as its very essence the temporary relief from responsibility and work, in the sense that only one who works can have a holiday. It would imply something very different from the play of children which we understand to be turned inward, as are dreams, for the working over of internal conflicts.

The distinction between co-operation in analysis and self-analytic work helps us to answer the question of when the individual's worklife begins. Its coincidence with the onset of latency will be discussed later in 'The pedagogic implications of sexual theory'. In agreement with Freud, my conception of the beginning of the adult part of the personality would coincide with the movement toward the resolutions of the Oedipus complex

1 Extract from the chapter of this name in *Sexual States of Mind* (1973).

in favour of introjective identification. While it is true that the resolution at latency is both incomplete in mechanism – hedged by repression and obsessional control – as well as in scope (largely pregenital in content), nonetheless the structuralisation of the super-ego-ideal from the multiplicity of part- and whole-objects in psychic reality is considerably forwarded at this time.

This massive movement toward introjective identification at latency utilises, of course, a mechanism that has been employed from the earliest times, for every movement from paranoid-schizoid to depressive position (Ps↔D) involves a movement toward introjective as against projective modes of identification.

I hope I may be forgiven for quoting again the stirring passage from 'The economic problem of masochism':

> The course of childhood development leads to an ever-increasing detachment from parents, and their personal significance for the super-ego recedes into the background. To the imagos they leave behind there are then linked the influences of teachers and authorities, self-chosen models and publicly recognised heroes, whose figures need no longer be introjected by an ego which has become more resistant. The last figure in the series that began with the parents is the dark power of Destiny which only the fewest of us are able to look upon as impersonal [i.e., death].

This point, that new qualities become linked to the images of the parents but that the figures of the newer influences need not be introjected, has been discussed earlier. The introjective basis of adult bisexuality was described for the purpose of distinguishing its polymorphism from that of infantile sexuality and of perversions respectively.

Here we have a different task in hand: namely to explain why adult work is so sexual, why the infantile organisation has an aversion to work and why the concept of sublimation has become redundant in the 'structural' era of psychoanalytic history. It must be kept in mind always that we are speaking of adult organisation of the personality and not of 'grown-up' individuals: in other words, that we are using the term metapsychologically, neither descriptively nor phenomenologically. We must relate play to work by placing each in turn in its relevant organisation. Later, the concept of perversion, in symptom and character, will be discussed in chapters on 'Tyranny' and 'Pornography'. What we must demonstrate, or rather elucidate, is that the infantile organisation of the self places the ego in a primary relation to the id, resulting in play, while the adult organisation of the self, through introjective identification, places the adult portion of the ego, in children and grown-ups alike, in a secondary relation to the id via the super-ego-ideal, resulting behaviourally in work.

The first part of our task has been done by Freud implicitly in all his theoretical formulations, whether structural or pre-structural, and regardless of the theory of instincts or of anxiety, memory, thinking, or of economic principles, whether pleasure, reality or repetition compulsion. His picture of the plight of the ego in 'The ego and the id' serving three masters – the id, the superego and the outside world – is indeed an accurate picture of the infantile organisation. What it perhaps does not make sufficiently clear are the economic aspects, which could only be elucidated by the next step in the discovery of economic principles of the mind, Melanie Klein's description of the paranoid-schizoid and depressive positions.

Her work demonstrated that the process of 'idealisation' involved more than what Freud had described as an object being 'aggrandised or exalted in the subject's mind'. She showed that a process of splitting-and-idealisation is involved, whereby all aspects of the object connected with mental pain are split-off as 'bad', leaving an 'idealised' object. This is not the same as a 'good' object, for its qualities so transcend the category of 'human' as to imply a persecutory demand for perfection. In other words, idealised objects present very little of that quality of forgiveness under which infantile thought-in-action, which we know as play, may proceed.

Where objects are still too idealised, confusion between good and bad may easily result, just as when conversely the splitting-and-idealisation is not adequate and fails to produce a clear distinction, in both self and objects. Under these circumstances play is not able to proceed because of excesses of persecutory anxiety and is either inhibited or replaced by concrete behaviour which is play-like in form but joyless and compulsive in quality. Delusions of identity due to narcissistic identifications, especially projective identifications, mar the childish spontaneity and inventiveness which the generosity and forgiving nature of good objects allow.

Under this hovering benevolence, the play of infantile structures enjoys an immunity from responsibility that enables the infantile ego to devote itself, in full egocentricity, to its developmental problems. The task of self-forgiveness, which is such a difficult one for the adult organisation when it does damage through mistakes of judgement, episodes of ill-will, negligence or ignorance in the outside world, is unknown to the infantile organisation, which finds total absolution in the tolerance of good objects and their reparative omnipotence in psychic reality. But just as psychic reality is primary and overwhelming in importance for the infantile structures, external reality and responsibility for the world becomes primary for the adult portion of the personality, in its introjective identification.[2]

Taken in this fuller sense Freud's description [of work and libido] in *Civilization and its Discontents* [*SE*, 21: 80 fn] acquires a richer meaning in which the pleasure of work need no longer be viewed as desexualised in any sense. Through the operation of admiration and introjection the 'existing inclination' and 'constitutionally reinforced impulses' have found their rightful place in personality structure, as the qualities of the superego, unique to the individual. Just as adult and infantile sexual behaviour can often not be distinguished descriptively, but only through analysis of unconscious phantasy and motivation, so work can often not be distinguished from pseudo-work, compulsion, infantile omnipotent control and other forms of non-play emergent in behaviour when infantile – rather than adult – organisation has taken control of motility. No descriptive criteria will help the analyst to recognise these aspects of acting-out and acting-in of his patient, or of himself. Only the analytic method of investigating transference and countertransference can help.

In the implication that all work is sexual in its meaning, we must acknowledge the affective aspect fully: namely, passion. Its differentiation from the excitement of infantile sexuality is again too utterly subjective and solipsistic to allow descriptive distinction, but in our metapsychological language we may try

---

2 See my dialogue with Adrian Stokes in *Painting and the Inner World* (1963) [author's note].

to use these terms precisely, and further distinguish passion from fanaticism, rage, ecstasy, and other categories of mental pleasure, as has been done in the gradual elucidation of the many types of mental pain.

In the structural theory the affects may be given their proper place in the functioning of the ego and are no longer necessarily linked with the id and mental energy. Their quantitative manipulation as an overriding principle ('Nirvana Principle') is replaced by their being subsumed under all three levels of economics (repetition compulsion, pleasure-pain-reality principle, and paranoid-schizoid-depressive positions). The concept of sublimation, whether as a poetical image ('refinement of memory'), a mechanism of defence (linked to reaction formation and desexualisation), or a consequence of superego harshness, is no longer needed as part of our metapsychological system of notation. It may be retained descriptively, perhaps, to indicate those aspects of behaviour where sexual aim and object are obscure without the aid of psychoanalytical investigation of the unconscious motivation and phantasy upon which they are founded. Indeed, the term 'sublimation' has long ago slipped through our scientific fingers and into general parlance, where its rather vague usage, sometimes implying a background of impotence or incapacity in sexual relations, does violence to Freud's original meaning as well as to later usage.

Just as Freud, in his later work, demonstrated the utility of the extension, in breadth and depth, of the term 'sexual' which he had proposed in the *Three Essays*, our psychoanalytic discoveries have now brought us to an even wider and most unexpected meaning of the word. As Freud's original neurophysiological frame of reference changed to a purely psychological one, the quasi-physiological idea of 'psychic energy' has needed to be replaced by purely mental concepts of 'meaning' and 'vitality'. While the vitality of infantile structures is derived from the id and is manifest as resulting from the play of conflict among the parts produced by primal splitting-and-idealisation and defensive splitting-and-projective-identification, the vitality of the adult part of the personality is dependent for its stability and availability upon the vitality of the internal objects. In its introjective identification with these internal parents, its bisexuality operates in the outside world at various levels of abstraction, but always with the same fundamental meaning – *parental*. This is reflected in our language usage of terms such as mother, father, child, motherhood, brainchild, seminal influence, creative, nurturing – and above all, love.

What is true at the basic level of individual sexual behaviour is also true in the realm of character: narcissistic identifications (infantile imitation and perverse caricaturing) together with adult introjective identifications shape the actual behaviour of individuals in the world. Small wonder that the individual person is so complex, so defiant of nosological pigeon-holing, so unpredictable.

CHAPTER EIGHTEEN

Intrusive identification and the Claustrum[1]

(1990)

In 1946 Mrs Klein presented this amazingly modest paper called 'Notes on some schizoid mechanisms' in which she described her discovery of the phenomenology of splitting processes and projective identification. At that time she was describing it as a very psychotic mechanism, seen in very ill people, and involving narcissistic identification with external objects. It was in fact the first description of the mechanism or the phantasy behind the narcissistic identifications, although Freud had used the term 'narcissistic identification'. Abraham had also used it, and gave it some substance in relation to manic-depressive states, but not as a description that was visible in ordinary personality functioning.

Now this first description by Mrs Klein, that was a of a very psychotic operation with external objects, very soon became recognised as operating with internal objects as well, and it became apparent that it added a new dimension to what Mr Money-Kyrle (1961) called 'man's picture of his world': that is, it opened up the prospect of people living in a world inside an object, adding another dimension to what was already the

---

1   A talk given in Lisbon c.1990, provided by Joao Sousa Monteiro.

two worlds that we live in, which Mrs Klein had defined as very concretely the internal world – not just the world of phantasy, but a very concrete internal world – and the external world, there was now added this third dimension of the world *inside* objects, both external and internal. The concept of projective identification quite enthralled her followers, and its development was also connected with her description of envy as an infantile emotional state that had very big consequences for development and for the analytical process.

The interest in projective identification, partly because of the emphasis that Mrs Klein herself laid upon it, was with the identificatory aspects of projective identification: that is, the way in which it brings about *instantaneously* a change in the person's sense of identity, an instantaneous identification with the mental state and the attributes and capabilities of the object with which is identified. This immediacy of identification enabled therefore a very clear distinction from the process that Freud had described of introjective identification, which he also saw as resulting in the differentiation between ego and superego, and a process between the two of them, essential for maturation. Introjective identification meant the internalisation into internal objects of certain qualities which then become the object of admiration and aspiration in the slow process of development.

Narcissistic identifications, of which the first description is Mrs Klein's description of projective identification, are immediate and produce an immediate sense of a change in identity. Some years later, Mrs Esther Bick described a second mechanism of narcissistic identification, which she called 'adhesive identification', which was a method of sticking on to the surface of an object and acquiring a sense of having its surface attributes. But projective identification was quite different; it involved an intrusion inside the object – in what Mrs Klein called an 'omnipotent phantasy' – by which the person had a sense of acquiring the qualities and capabilities of the character and personality, not just their appearance.

It was soon recognised that the identificatory part of projective identification was only one side of the identificatory part of the phenomenology of projective identification. But there was another side to it, which was the projective part, or the intrusive part. The experience of the world inside the object: the claustro-phobic world. Now, the experience of this differentiation between the identificatory and the projective phenomenology consequent to projective identification gradually produced a whole spectrum of new understandings, both of psychopathology and of the devel-opmental process. It became clear, for instance, that the process of projective identification with internal objects was at least as important, if not more important, in developmental processes, than identification with external objects. It also became clear that the method of intrusion inside the object was not always an active intrusion: that it could be a passive intrusion, a kind of being swallowed up, enveloped into projective identification. So the phenomenology related to projective identification is therefore divisible in various dimensions: the dimension of objects (internal and external) that are the object of identification; the dimension of the differentiation between the identificatory part and the projective part; and the dimension of its occurrence as either an active intrusion, or a passive enveloping or swallowing up.

In the clinical phenomenology this concept highlights partic-ularly the ways in which splitting processes and projective identi-fication operate together – that is, part of a personality may exist inside an object, and another part of the personality outside. Or the intrusion may be a temporary one – the person may enter into the object and then come out again. There's also the implica-tion that the two may exist simultaneously and that conscious-ness may be dominated by one or the other, alternating. You get material from a patient that first indicates his identificatory processes, and a few minutes or a few sessions later you get mate-rial indicating the projective or claustrophobic aspect.

So, this concept, and the recognition of its complexities, made it possible to follow clinical material in ways that had seemed utterly chaotic previously. With that advance in the ability of the analyst to follow the material of the patient (which, I must say, was always clearer with children than with adults) the ability to follow the material more closely, and to not be enveloped by the confusion that the patient is enveloped by, made it possible to study some of the other particularities of the phenomenology of projective identification – both the identificatory aspects and the projective aspects.

The realisation that grew out of work with children and particularly with autistic children, or children emerging from autism, was that the inside of the object, particularly the maternal object, is compartmentalised, and that the different compartments have different qualities and different significance, and also are entered in phantasy through different orifices: in the most pathological manifestations, the mother's rectum – at best a sort of rubbish tip, at worst a concentration camp. Then, there seems to be a another fairly distinct and demarcated compartment corresponding to the entry through the vagina, which is a place of intense sexual excitement, and a kind of sexual elitism as well. And thirdly there is a compartment that is up in the breasts, or in the mother's head, or both, or the 'head-breast' as we came to talk about it, which is a place of utter comfort, safety, and abundance; but also a place, in its identificatory aspects, of intense elitism, sense of superiority, of expanded and almost universal knowledge, based on the sort of poverty of imagination that can only see one thing, and therefore feels certain that that is the truth – that kind of one-track-minded omniscience. It is a place which generates indolence, complacency, and the sense of superiority that came to be known as 'pseudomaturity'.

Now, it is the study of this compartmentalising, to which this last book on the Claustrum is devoted (1992), which seems to me to have thrown so much light on the different aspects of psychopathology in children, and the ways in which they are augmented and evolved in adolescence and in the major steps in development from infancy to childhood, childhood to school-life, school-life to puberty and adolescence: the ways in which they are variously interfered with by the activity of projective identification. The recognition of the compartmentalisation of the mother's inside throws a lot of light on these things. Now, I say 'inside the mother' because this seems to be the main object of projective identificatory phantasies – the maternal object. However, there are situations in which identifications with the father are also very intense, particularly identifications at a very part-object level with his penis and its functions inside the mother. That aspect of projective identification is relatively transitory because its purpose is mainly to find a vehicle for entry into the mother, so that in both types of projective identification, entry into the mother is really the ultimate aim of these phantasies. Entry into the mother, possession of the spaces inside her, and of the maternal characteristics and qualities and capabilities.

Now, to turn to the role of projective identification generally in the development of children, and then to pass on to its role in the psychopathology of childhood. It seems to me to be quite evident now that projective identification phantasies are ubiquitous, that they play some role in the development of every person, but that they do not form in any sense a phase in development. Projective identification is a phantasy that has mental consequences which are primarily modulating: their intention is to modulate mental pain. It does not constitute a phase in development, but runs through development as a modulating device, modulating mental pain. The next thing to recognise about it is that it is most particularly employed to modulate the mental pain of separation from the mother. It does therefore tend to start very early in infancy, and is of course employed in proportion to what one might call the insensitivity of the mother to the child's separation anxieties. This you can see very clearly in baby observation: the difference between a mother who is sensitive and a mother who is insensitive. A mother who puts down the baby and walks into the kitchen and out of the baby's sight, and goes about her business in the kitchen, and does not pay any attention to the baby until it starts crying or screaming is very different from a mother who as she walks away is talking to the baby; while she is in the kitchen out of the baby's sight she is still talking to the baby, or singing for the baby and so on: she maintains her contact with the baby, both in her mind and in communication. This is why I say that the insensitivity of the mother to the baby's distress in separation plays a very important role in determining the baby's use of projective identificatory phantasies for modulating the pain of separation.

Now, it would seem, both in the study of children and from the dreams of adult patients, that the most common phantasy that involves projective identification with the mother as an external object involves the baby seeing the mother walking away. At a level of partial objects, the mother turning her back and walking away has the significance of her two breasts turning into her two buttocks, and the baby's intrusive phantasy is to enter into her anus to get inside her once again, to go with her in its phantasy. Of course, what happens is that this occurs internally and the baby's state of mind becomes dominated by the phantasy of being inside the mother and going away with her. The result is that the baby does not cry, and when the mother comes back she finds that the baby does not make contact with her, but is busy playing with its fingers, paying with its toys, ignores her and so one. The contact with the external object has been broken because the baby has now entered into his internal object and is feeling grown-up, independent, absorbed in its interesting enquiries into how its fingers work and so on and so forth. That seems to be the most ubiquitous projective identificatory phantasy: of entering into the anus and rectum of the mother as she walks away, but it also has very pathological consequences which I will come to in a moment.

The next most ubiquitous projective identificatory phantasies involving separation are the phantasies of the pregenital Oedipus complex: phantasies related to the parents being together and united in some sexual way, which the baby naturally interprets in the light of its own pregenital preoccupations. That is, that the parents are really viewed as feeding on or as excreting into one another's bodies, in either an oral or in an anal way; and the baby's projective identification – either because it is sleeping in the same room and feels intensely involved in their sexuality, or because it is separated in another room and hears evidences of their sexuality – leads it either to projective identification with its father's penis entering into the mother, or intrusion into the mother's vagina participating in the sexual intercourse. This pregenital operation of projective identification then of course may become more genital in the genital Oedipus complex later in early childhood, at the age of four, five, six and so on. But it tends to preserve its pregenital implications, and therefore colours the genital Oedipus complex very strongly with these oral and anal implications, which are intensified by the employment of projective identification.

Pathological identification

Now, all this I have been talking is within the range of normal development. I will now talk a few minutes about its extension or aggravation or amplification as pathology. I will start with the description the psychopathology of projective identification as seen in work with children. One can see very clearly in baby observation and in the observation of young children, the immediacy of the baby's identification with the mother's activities – her moods, her emotions, and so on. The other day, in a baby observation group, it was described that the baby had a little rash on its face (this was a baby just short of one year of age, already walking, already clearly understanding language, to a very great extent) and the mother brought her eyes very close to the baby's cheek to look at his little rash, and as soon as she did so, the baby walked across to a bookshelf on which there were little ceramic figures, and one after another he picked up these figures and looked at them very carefully and put them down. I mean, you can see that immediate identification with the mother, carrying out the actions and suffused with the mother's intense concentration, but of course not implemented in a way that had the same meaning as the mother. This is a very important thing: that the emotions and the actions coming from projective identification with the mother's mind (for the baby also her breasts) are closely conjoined. The mood, the emotions, the actions that come from projective identification have all the *appearance* of being meaningful, but in fact are relatively empty of meaning.

Pseudomaturity one can see starting as early as one year of age, like with this child I just described. There is a lovely paper about it in the book on *Studies in Extended Metapsychology* [1986], called 'A one-year-old goes to nursery', which is a wonderful description by a child psychiatrist, Romana Negri in Milan, of a one-year-old going to nursery school because his mother returned to work, and of the terrible separation anxieties that the baby had, which turned into pseudomaturity the moment the mother left the child in the nursery. In an instant the baby became totally socialised, and one of the staff. Not one of the children – he became one of the staff. One year of age! An amazing description, I recommend it to you.

Probably the most common form of psychopathology that we meet with in both children and adults in the relatively middle-class population that is served by psychoanalysis, is pseudomaturity. Now, this form of psychopathology, of the crystallising of character around projective identification with the intelligent, attentive and caring qualities of the parents (usually the mother, but sometimes mother and father combined) produces a simulation of maturity, and is often accompanied by a capacity for a limited kind of learning, a kind of soaking up of information, and therefore a very adequate school performance in most school systems. A child can find a way to be a very successful student simply by sponging up, soaking up information. This pseudomaturity leads to very successful social adaptation, but to inevitably deteriorating intimate relationships. And although we see children brought occasionally because their parents have recognised that this child has established a premature independence, usually we only see it in adult patients in their thirties, who are socially successful and whose intimate relationships are crumbling or almost non-existent. As I say, it consists of what Bion would call a carapace or shell – a social façade of maturity, competence, humanist values, etcetera, based on a projective identification that starts very early in childhood, as early as one year of age or even earlier. But most characteristically it starts at the toilet-training period, after weaning, when weaning and toilet-training catch the child in a sort of crossfire of anxiety. Projective identification is invoked and the child becomes clean and dry and independent, and no longer needs a mother or a father, and therefore is in a position to be very helpful to mummy, to be mummy's little assistant with the next babies, and to be amazingly immune to jealousy of the younger children; and it is only the sensitive parent who realises that the child has become joyless and lacks the colourfulness of childhood. It can be recognised in that way, but unfortunately, most parents are delighted with this helpful and easy child who you can leave with neighbours, who you can park with grandma or grandpa, and so on, and rest assured that they won't make a fuss.

So, pseudomaturity, starting very early, is probably the most frequent psychopathological form of projective identification that we see in psychoanalytic work, both with children and with adults.

The problems of analysis of pseudomaturity are primarily the analysis of this independence and sense of self-sufficiency and wisdom, due to limited imagination and what I call one-track-mindedness. The arrangement of the compartments of the inside of the mother's body are such that they lead into one another: that is, a part of the personality living in projective identification with the head-breast and being very superior and elitist and independent may, under the pressure of sexual desire, slide down into the genital area and become nymphomaniac, have explosions of erotic desire, and be quite overwhelmed by them. This also happens in childhood, with children becoming suddenly tremendously erotic and seductive with other children and with adult figures, and it plays an important part in the psychopathology of the sexuality of children, which in our country (in England, at present) has reached a kind of epidemic proportion.

One does not know whether it is epidemic amongst the social workers seeing it, or an epidemic amongst the adults being worried about it, or whether it is actually an epidemic between children with one another or with adult figures. But the problem of what is called sexual abuse has become a very prominent problem in English educational and social circles. And projective identification plays a very big part in this. When children are in projective identification with the parents' sexuality on this very pregenital level that I have discussed with you, they are not only seductive but very vulnerable to seduction by other children or adult figures, and it is in this area that brother-sister incest, and father-daughter incest, but also father-son incest not only comes into existence, but it perpetuated. I mean, that is the problem with the child abusers: not a so-called traumatic incident like one thinks about in Freudian terms – something that once happened and was left unconscious, etcetera. The problem with child abusers is that a relationship is established and goes on secretly for years, really. And the state of mind that is engendered by it (by a pseudomature mental state combined with an essentially pregenital sexuality that is experienced precociously as if it were fully mature) leads to prolonged sexual activities starting usually in the latency period, usually with an older sibling, sometimes with a parent figure. Although generally, one assumes that for a parent to enter into a prolonged incestuous relationship they must be very psychotic or borderline psychotic, to begin with.

Now this whole area, that may explode in adolescence, is visible in earlier childhood. The areas of addiction and perversion seem

to be based on the operation of projective identification, particularly with the mother's rectum, the area that, as I say, varies from
being a rubbish tip to a concentration camp. This can usually be
seen to have started during the process of toilet training and to
involve secret erotic experiences of defaecation: of having a nappy
full of faeces, of sitting long hours on the toilet excluding and
then retracting the faeces in a masturbatory way; this leads on to
anal masturbatory habits, and very great secrecy, and to be largely
a consequence of the phantasy of projective identification into
the mother's rectum. It involves, of course, a great deal of erotisation of the faeces – what we call the faecal penis – as an object
of erotic excitement and even of a kind of Dionysiac worship; it
involves an estimation of the preciousness of the faeces, as being
the contents of the mother's body, that can be stolen and are of
limitless commercial value. But most important of all, it involves
sadomasochism. The basis of sadomasochism seems to have to
do with this area of the mother's body, which is viewed as a very
particular world that is structured very much like institutions or
structures in the outside world – that is, hierarchic, with levels
of authority and privilege superimposed upon one another. But
of course this hierarchic structure when managed humanely in
the outside world is essentially one of tyranny and submission;
but in this interior world of the mother's rectum, it is, in its most
ghastly form, the concentration camp.

The concentration camp is a marvellous model for this
perversion: for the basic, fundamental perversion, in which
what should be love-making and making babies is turned into
sadomasochism and the killing of babies. This can be seen to
start very early in childhood. Very often it seems to involve not
just anal preoccupation but anal masturbation, and manifests
itself symptomatically really only in childhood; even quite small
children make it into actual sadomasochistic behaviour with one
another of a very secret sort, particularly when parents are not
vigilant about the children's activities with one another or with
their friends. The basic structure of tyranny and submission
plays a big part in many children's lives, partly in the pathology of aggressiveness toward other children, but probably more
frequently in the form of submissiveness and timidity, not just
in boys but in girls. You can say to a child: but why do you play

with him? He's always hurting you. 'He is my friend!' It is the sort of pathology where the child cannot distinguish between admiration and submission, and the masochism is evident in the behaviour. But it is only in puberty and adolescence that it breaks out and takes a manifest social orientation, mostly in the form of homosexual perversity in boys, prostitution phantasies and enactment in the girls, and the drug-taking.

This then is a sort of spectrum of the psychopathology of projective identification that as I say becomes most obvious in adolescence. The pseudomaturity becomes most obvious in early childhood and extends through to mid-life, and then there are the serious illnesses based on projective identification.

Addendum

Part-object relationships

When you recognise part-object relationships you immediately recognise how reversible they are by projective identification, and this is something one sees in children all the time, how quickly they reverse the relationship, so that the abandoner is the abandoned, or the seducer is the seduced, or the attacker is the attacked, and so on. That reversibility is a characteristic of part-object relationships.

The seductiveness of the Claustrum

The ordinary way a young child tolerates separation is by turning to its internal objects – for instance, when it puts its thumb in its mouth. This is quite a different thing from using the internal objects as a refuge, which one sees in the projective identificatory process. So that the situation I described of the mother walking away and being insensitive to the baby's feelings, is not really a turning to an internal object, but an intrusive phantasy into an external object that is immediately accompanied by an internal process: as soon as the mother disappears round the corner, it continues with the internal object. So that one in the case of projective processes one cannot speak about being attracted to the internal or attracted to the internal object: the attraction is to the *inside* of objects, to the world inside the object. That is the basis of the claustrophobia. The reason the claustrum seems to be closed and a place you cannot escape from is not because there is a closed door, but because the outside seems so threatening and unattractive compared to the inside.

In the course of the therapy of people who have been lost in projective identification, you find that they eventually agree to come out, but find the outside world so full of depressive pain that they rush back in again, and you get this isolating process from the world. So, it is not correct to speak of being attracted to the internal object; they are attracted to the inside of the object, whether internal or external. It is that world inside the object that is attractive.